929.
1
BES

Best, Laura.

Genealogy for the
first time.

| DATE | | | |
|---|---|---|---|
| | | | |
| | | | |
| | | | |
| | | | |
| | | | |
| | | | |
| | | | |
| | | | |
| | | | |
| | | | |
| | | | |
| | | | |
| | | | |
| | | | |

# Genealogy

# for the first time®

*Courtesy of Chris Little*

# Genealogy
## for the first time®

### research your family history

_Laura Best_

Sterling Publishing Co., Inc. New York

A Sterling/Chapelle Book

# Chapelle, Ltd.:

Jo Packham
Sara Toliver
Cindy Stoeckl

Editor: Laura Best
Editorial Director: Caroll Shreeve
Art Director: Karla Haberstich
Copy Editor: Marilyn Goff
Graphics Illustrator: Kim Taylor
Photographer: Kevin Dilley, Hazen Photography
Photo Stylists: Suzy Skadburg, Laura Best
Staff: Burgundy Alleman, Areta Bingham, Ray Cornia,
Emily Frandsen, Lana Hall, Susan Jorgenson,
Barbara Milburn, Lecia Monsen,
Karmen Quinney, Desirée Wybrow

If you have any questions or comments, please contact:
Chapelle, Ltd., Inc.,
P.O. Box 9252, Ogden, UT 84409
(801) 621-2777 • (801) 621-2788 Fax
e-mail: chapelle@chapelleltd.com
web site: chapelleltd.com

*George & Barbara Hennessey, 1936*

Library of Congress Cataloging-in-Publication Data

Best, Laura.
   Genealogy for the first time : research your family history / Laura Best.
       p. cm.
   "A Sterling/Chapelle book."
   Includes bibliographical references (p.   ) and index.
   ISBN 1-4027-0109-8
   1. Genealogy. 2. United States--Genealogy--Handbooks, manuals, etc.
I. Title.
CS16.B46 2003
929.1--dc21

2003005528

10 9 8 7 6 5 4 3 2 1

Published by Sterling Publishing Co., Inc.
387 Park Avenue South, New York, NY 10016
©2003 by Laura Best
Distributed in Canada by Sterling Publishing
c/o Canadian Manda Group, One Atlantic Avenue, Suite 105
Toronto, Ontario, Canada M6K 3E7
Distributed in Great Britain by Chrysalis Books
64 Brewery Road, London N7 9NT, England
Distributed in Australia by Capricorn Link (Australia) Pty. Ltd.
P.O. Box 704, Windsor, NSW 2756, Australia
Printed in China
All Rights Reserved
Sterling ISBN 1-4027-0109-8

*Constance Sophia Miller, 1904*

*above:* Constance Miller Flygare (1903–1992) stands next to a chair made from the wooden driver's seat of the wagon that brought her pioneer ancestors west in 1851.

*right:* As an adult, Constance made the needlepoint seat cushion which is currently on the chair. This chair has been passed down from mother to daughter for five generations—keeping the spirit of their pioneer heritage alive.

*Courtesy of Carolyn Gillette Apsley*
*Granddaughter of Constance Miller Flygare*

# Table of Contents

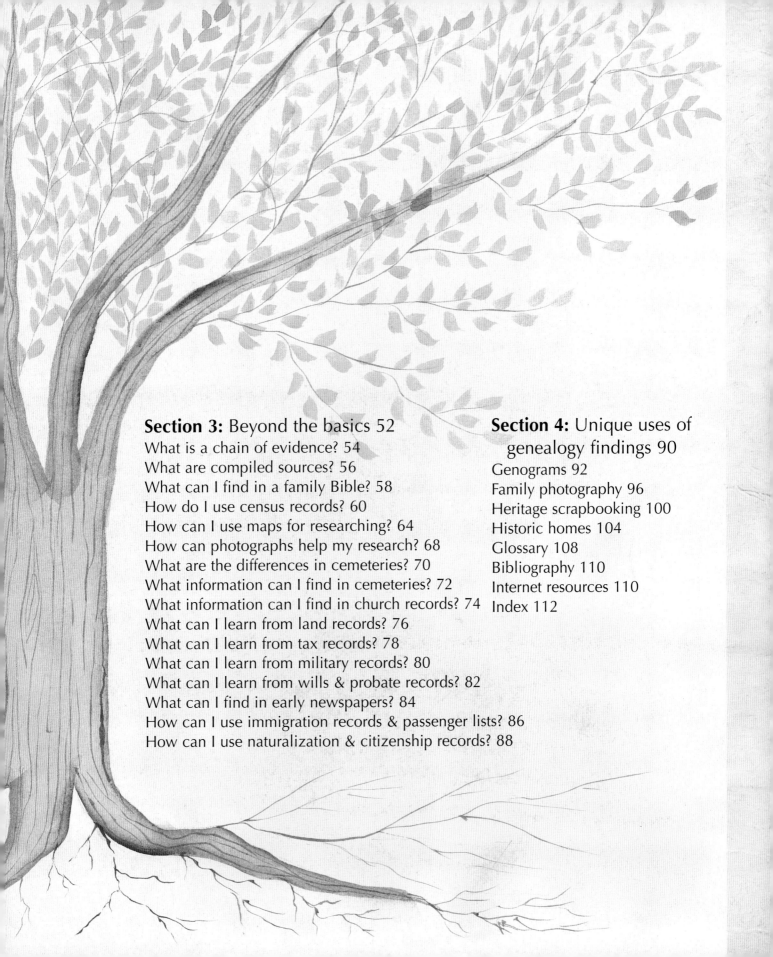

# Genealogy for the first time

## Introduction

Millions of people are actively engaged in some form of family research. Whether acquiring a sense of belonging or discovering a link to a hero lost in battle, various reasons are cited for people's fascination with their ancestors. For many, what starts as a simple curiosity, grows into an obsession.

Genealogy is not merely the gathering of names, dates, and places; nor is it meant to exclusively look for the kings and queens in one's lineage. While those things are important and represent the framework of family history, serious genealogists are more concerned with finding the story of a family's past.

A person searches for his past family members in order to learn of and record the unique and authentic lives of those who formed his heritage. To do this, a researcher must possess a certain degree of passion for the truth, a knowledge of the information sources available, and an ability to evaluate the facts he finds.

There are a number of sources and resources to explore while researching, the basics of which are addressed in this book. As you research, it is important to strive for the quality of information you collect, not the quantity.

Additionally, genealogists cannot learn too much of the history and geography of where their forefathers lived and traveled, the social customs, the events behind their family's actions, their occupational trials, and their family's joys and sorrows. Discovering this type of family history helps anchor your sense of belonging in the world.

*Phoebe Louisa Richardson Miller, 1876–1958*

8

*Ichabod Ennis & Ennis Adams, 1910*

## How to use this book

The purpose of this book is to inspire and encourage people who are interested in researching their heritage to begin the journey. Expertise is not required, but a desire to learn, research, and persevere is needed. Rewarding results can be achieved if you are willing to experiment a little and use your imagination.

For the person who is interested in genealogy or family history for the first time, this book provides a basic guide to the primary methods and sources used in genealogy work.

**Section 1** helps you discover what information is already available to you.

**Section 2** tells you how to organize, record, and store the information you discover.

**Section 3** teaches you more-advanced techniques of finding information first hand.

**Section 4** presents unique ways in which experienced genealogists have preserved and used their findings.

Many thanks to these professionals who have contributed photographs and shared samples of their research.

*George T. & Fanny Standifird Hennessey, 1935*

*Ethel, Clemence, George & John Miller, 1885*

*Courtesy of M. Finkel & Daughter*

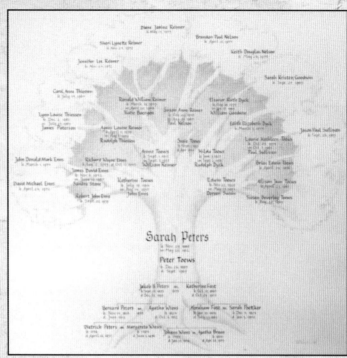

*Courtesy of Susan A. Nelson*

*Courtesy of Cynthia Gessel Gaufin*

*Courtesy of Areta Bingham*

*Courtesy of Susan A. Nelson*

*Section 1:*
*Genealogy basics*

# Where do I start?

Genealogy is, metaphorically speaking, one large puzzle. You may pick up the pieces in any order to place them. However, some pieces will be more difficult to place than others and may need to be set aside until other pieces are fitted together to give better reference and framework.

When putting a puzzle together, one normally begins with the easiest pieces such as the border or a certain object in the puzzle with distinctive color and shape. When doing family research, or genealogy, this is comparable to recording the facts you already know or finding the information that is easily obtainable.

The second attempt at the puzzle is placing puzzle pieces of medium difficulty such as trees, a house, or a ship. The genealogy equivalent to this would entail conducting personal interviews, searching obituaries, and locating vital records.

The final attempt at fleshing out your family's history can be compared to placing the most difficult pieces of a puzzle, such as the sky or ocean. Your ancestor may have changed his name or there may be more than one person with your relative's name living in the same area. As with piecing together the sky of a puzzle, some experimenting, searching, and assessing is involved in finding the right members of your family.

To be certain your "puzzle pieces" end up in the proper positions, use genealogy charts and forms to record your findings. (See What is a pedigree chart? on pages 32–33 and What is a family group sheet? on pages 36–37.)

Family of Henry Edward, 1875–1973 &
Lillie Adams Hennessey, 1884–1971

# What information do I already have?

Gather together any information in your possession which documents the names, dates, places, and activities of your family. Do not try to do this in a day. Take your time. Rummage through the various places in your home containing your life's memorabilia and place these treasures in a conveniently located box or area.

Involve your parents, siblings, and children in this gathering. Collect certificates, journals, scrapbooks, old letters, family Bibles, school records, military records, obituaries, deeds and wills, photographs, applications for lineage societies, newspaper clippings, funeral cards, account books, baby books, Christmas lists, address books, needlepoint samplers—any article which gives factual information about your family members.

Years ago, letters announced the news of births, deaths, and marriages. Today, sources such as scrapbooks and baby books may include newspaper clippings, photographs, places of residence, important events, and other genealogical data. Information on living family members, such as your children and grandchildren, is just as important as that of your great grandparents.

Gather together photographs—even if you do not know who is in them. Your future research may identify those in the photographs.

Whether or not you think the information is important, collect all the documentation you can into a centrally located area. This process may take some time, so keep your found objects in secure boxes until you can begin sorting.

Set aside a work space to spread out papers, books, and documents. Though this space can be your kitchen table or a designated area of your den, keep the area clutter-free, well stocked with permanent ink pens and notebooks, and accessible to the records and documents you will accumulate.

A computer will be invaluable in your researching and storing of information. (See How can a computer help my research? on pages 44–45.)

Secure a box or filing cabinet and some manila folders for sorting and storing accumulated materials. You will refer back to various forms and documents as you piece together your family tree. These valuable documents may include irreplaceable photographs. (See How can photographs help my research? on pages 68–69.) Keeping your work area organized and clean will help protect your documents and keep you focused on your work.

As you accumulate documents and records, write down personal information for which you have proven documentation. Oftentimes, people make mistakes when they try to give information from memory, such as the death dates of their grandparents, birth dates of their children, and information about their parents. Since family knowledge is subject to the fallibility and fickleness of memory, it is advisable to check and verify facts by the use of public or official records. Even the simplest information such as your own birth date and the places where you have lived will eventually need to be documented. Use a form, such as the Information I Already Have on page 17, to show at a glance what you are lacking and who may have the information you need.

Eventually, you will use the information you collect to fill out the basic records kept by genealogists. The pedigree chart lists a person and their direct ancestors along with pertinent data on their life. (See What is a pedigree chart? on pages 32–33.) The family group sheet places families in units along with their vital facts. (See What is a family group sheet? on pages 36–37.)

# Information I Already Have

| | Complete name | Birth date | Birth place | Marriage date | Marriage place | Death date | Death place | Person/place most likely to have information you are missing: |
|---|---|---|---|---|---|---|---|---|

Your name:

_____ ▪ ▪ ▪ ▪ ▪

Your parents' names:

_____ ▪ ▪ ▪ ▪ ▪ ▪ ▪     _____

_____ ▪ ▪ ▪ ▪ ▪ ▪ ▪     _____

Your grandparents' names:

_____ ▪ ▪ ▪ ▪ ▪ ▪ ▪     _____

_____ ▪ ▪ ▪ ▪ ▪ ▪ ▪     _____

_____ ▪ ▪ ▪ ▪ ▪ ▪ ▪     _____

_____ ▪ ▪ ▪ ▪ ▪ ▪ ▪     _____

Your great-grandparents' names:

_____ ▪ ▪ ▪ ▪ ▪ ▪ ▪     _____

_____ ▪ ▪ ▪ ▪ ▪ ▪ ▪     _____

_____ ▪ ▪ ▪ ▪ ▪ ▪ ▪     _____

_____ ▪ ▪ ▪ ▪ ▪ ▪ ▪     _____

_____ ▪ ▪ ▪ ▪ ▪ ▪ ▪     _____

_____ ▪ ▪ ▪ ▪ ▪ ▪ ▪     _____

_____ ▪ ▪ ▪ ▪ ▪ ▪ ▪     _____

_____ ▪ ▪ ▪ ▪ ▪ ▪ ▪     _____

Fill in the information on the appropriate lines of the chart above. When you can document certain facts about each individual, such as a full name off of a birth certificate, check the box denoting that you already have that information. Blank boxes represent information you lack.

# What are primary & secondary sources?

A primary source is a record created at the time of an event, usually by someone with personal knowledge. A secondary source consists of documents, oral accounts, or any other record which was created sometime after the event took place or with information that was supplied by someone who was not an eyewitness to the event.

Vital records are the most common primary sources. These government documents record the most basic events of a person's life, such as birth, marriage, or death. While in the United States and Canada they are called "vital" records, in other countries they are listed as Civil Registration.

Be aware that vital documents may contain both primary and secondary information. For example, a death certificate is a primary record for a death date but a secondary source for a birth date since it was not recorded at the time of the birth. When finding conflicting information, remember that primary sources are normally more accurate than secondary records.

Each vital record has the potential of taking you back one more generation with new names. When linking families together, be certain to move backward in time from your parents to grandparents. If you jump ahead, you may introduce the wrong family into your records.

Birth records traditionally give name, sex, date, place of birth, and names of parents. These records sometimes also give the parents' birthplaces, ages, occupations, addresses, and the number of other children born.

Marriage certificates or licenses will differ in content, depending upon the information required by the locality which issued the license. Many provide only the date of the event and the name of the bride and groom. Some marriage records provide the couple's names, their ages, the names of their parents, and their parents' occupations. The addresses of the bride and groom

before their marriage are also significant. If either person was under age, the signature of the parent giving permission for the marriage will also be on the license.

By 1900, many states required the filing of a marriage license application, which typically asked for the place of birth, the place of residence, and the names of parents.

Some marriage records are simply notations made by the performing minister, who later stopped by the courthouse to report the event to the county clerk. In most states, marriage records are kept at the county level. Marriage records are usually found in the bride's county of residence.

Early death records provide the name, the death date and place, residence, and cause of death. More-recent records may also include names of parents, name of spouse, occupation, birth date, birth place, medical cause of death, age of the deceased, cemetery, and mortuary or funeral home. If death records are not available, cemetery records are a good substitute. (See What information can I find in cemeteries? on pages 72–73.)

If you know your ancestors were divorced, such records provide the names and ages of the petitioners, their birth places, addresses, occupations, names and ages of their children, joint property, and their grounds for divorce. Be aware, however, that these records are not always accessible.

Public records about yourself are available to

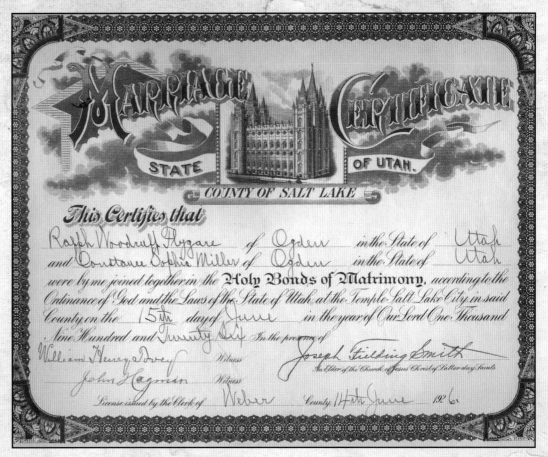

you because you have a right to that information. When you are making inquiries about others, even though they are related to you, you must consider privacy laws. Some states restrict records less than fifty years old. Even the census is kept private for two years. The Social Security Administration will furnish information about any deceased person regardless of relationship. Deceased people have no privacy rights, according to federal policies. But you do have to prove that the person about whom you are inquiring is deceased.

Release of information in private records is up to the record holder. The information held by funeral homes and privately owned cemeteries is considered private. They usually furnish information to genealogists about people for whom they have performed services, but they are under no obligation. Hospitals are also careful about releasing information that would violate a person's privacy.

*Courtesy of Connie Duran*

Courtesy of Connie Duran

## Section 2:
## Basic research techniques

# 1

*technique*

Use the following seven steps to complete a research cycle.

1. Consult your information sheet. (Refer to Information I Already Have on page 17.) Choose an ancestor and an event where information is missing. Set a goal to find this missing information.

2. Choose a record to search to reach your goal. (See Where can I find certain facts? on pages 26–27.)

3. Locate the record. (See How do I obtain information from my family? on pages 30–31.)

4. Transfer the new information onto your pedigree chart and family group sheets. (See What is a pedigree chart? on pages 32–33 and What is a family group sheet? on pages 36–37.)

5. Cite your sources. (See How do I cite my sources? on pages 40–41.)

6. Make a copy of the new document and file it. (See How should I file my findings? on pages 42–43.)

7. Evaluate the new information to determine whether or not it meets your goal. (See How do I evaluate my findings? on pages 38–39.) If the goal is not met, return to Step 2 above and choose a different record, then repeat Steps 3–7. If the information is sufficient, return to Step 1 and set a new goal.

## What are the basic steps of genealogy?

The first rule of genealogy is to work from information you already know. Taking a leap into the unknown past often leads to error, perhaps later leading to the discovery that you were tracing the wrong family. To avoid introducing a "puzzle piece" which does not belong, search on a step-by-step basis. Taking small steps at the beginning will lead to larger steps later.

Once you have recorded as much information as you know on your information sheet, it is time to begin your family research.

Gathering basic family history information consists of using a Genealogy Research Cycle as shown on page 23. Every time you repeat the cycle, you will learn more about the lives and times of your ancestors and be able to work those facts into a more complete family history.

Using this cycle, continue setting goals and researching those in your immediate family, then work backward to your parents, grandparents, and so forth. Continue moving around the cycle, discovering new information with each rotation.

# Genealogy Research Cycle

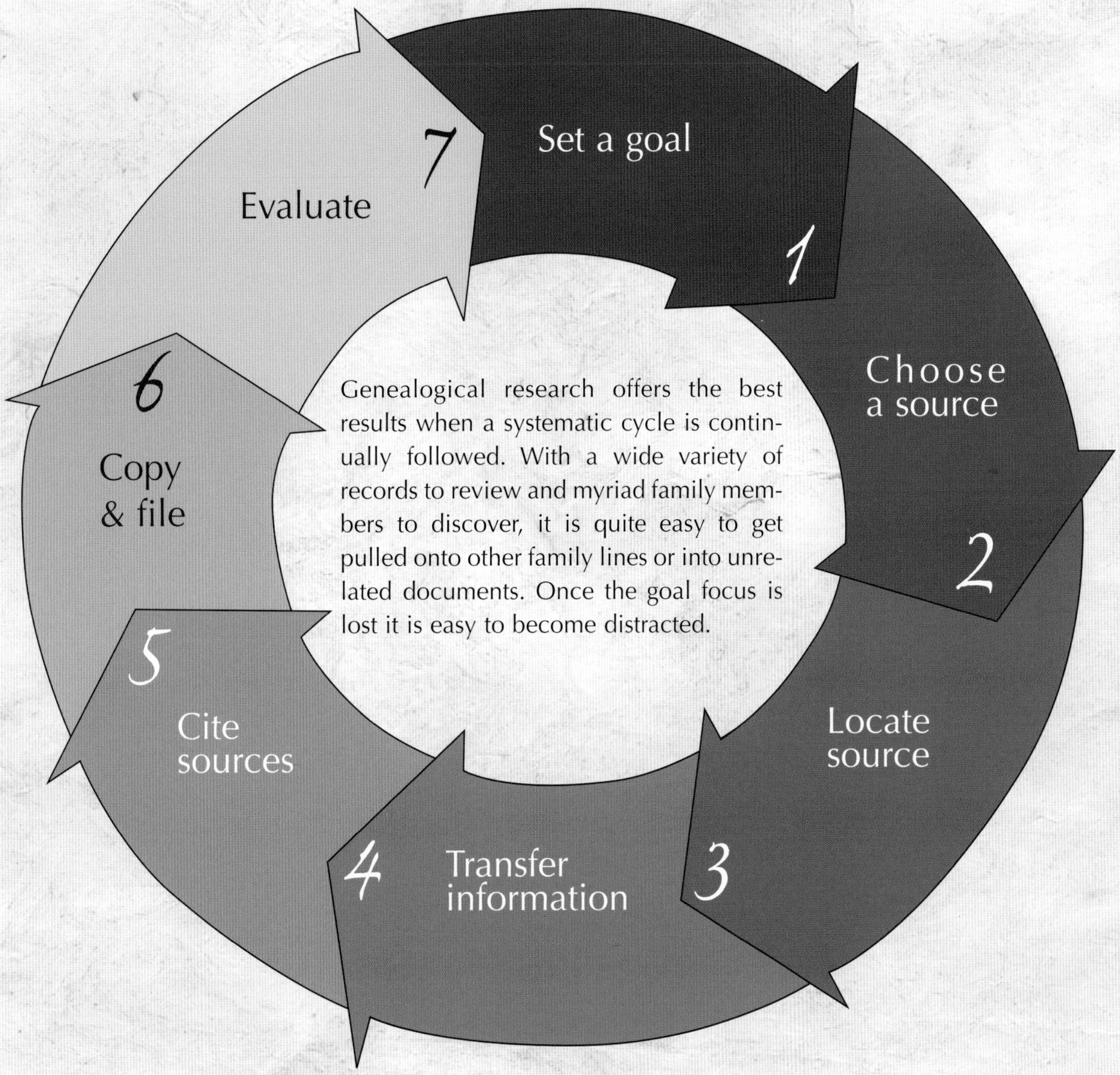

**Set a goal** *1*

**Choose a source** *2*

**Locate source** *3*

**Transfer information** *4*

**Cite sources** *5*

**Copy & file** *6*

**Evaluate** *7*

Genealogical research offers the best results when a systematic cycle is continually followed. With a wide variety of records to review and myriad family members to discover, it is quite easy to get pulled onto other family lines or into unrelated documents. Once the goal focus is lost it is easy to become distracted.

23

# 2
## technique

*Margaret Amelia Hanson Flygare and her sons, 1915*

Use the following four steps when setting a goal.

1. Be certain the information you currently have is correct. Building upon facts that are incorrect or inaccurate will affect further research. (Refer to Information I Already Have on page 17.)

2. Starting with the generation closest to you and working backward, choose an ancestor to learn more about.

3. Choose an event in their life that is missing. Select an ancestor about whom you already know something such as an approximate date of birth, marriage, or death, or where they lived. This is probably the most important step in the process because it will focus your search on only one question about one person at a time.

4. Be careful not to set your goal too high or too complex. Keep the question simple. Where was my father born? When did my grandparents marry? Certainly more information could come from the research. You may find where your grandparents were married when you locate the date.

## How do I start?

Genealogy is a process—not to be rushed. Each person, date, and place is to be accurately located and correctly recorded within a family group. Wonderful stories and interesting facts may surface as you find the basic facts about a family's life—such as the story behind the pet rooster in the photograph above.

Research in an orderly manner—working backward to find each individual. One of the best ways to find new information about parents or the next generation back is by searching for the children's vital records. For instance, if you do not know when your ancestor was married, find the birth date of the first child. The first child often came approximately one year after the marriage. This will give you the approximate date needed to search for the marriage records.

If you do not know where your ancestor lived, find out where his or her children were born or were married.

Depending on the goal and the missing information, different records and a variety of methods may be used. The Flowchart of the Research Process shown on page 25 gives an overall example of how you will make your way through a variety of records and methods while researching. Further instruction on these methods and records are discussed throughout this book.

# Flowchart of the Research Process

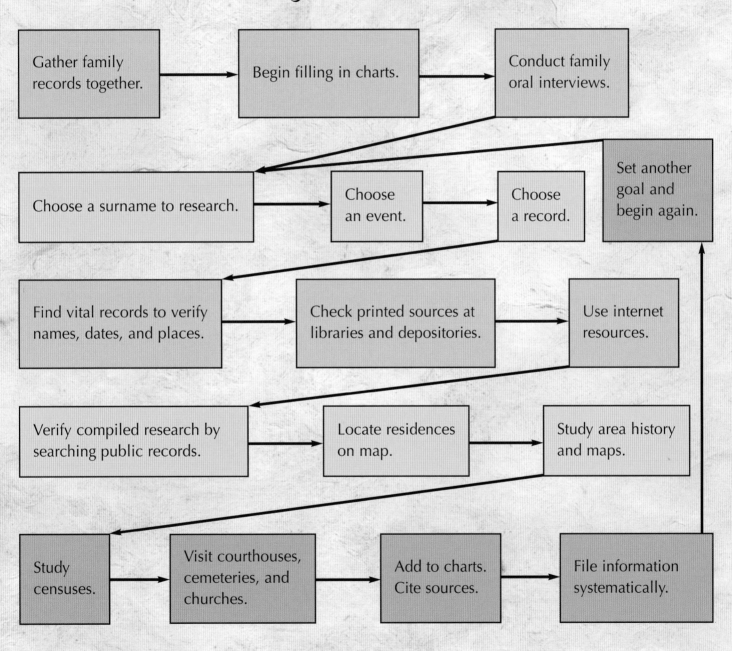

Gather family records together. → Begin filling in charts. → Conduct family oral interviews.

Choose a surname to research. → Choose an event. → Choose a record.

Set another goal and begin again.

Find vital records to verify names, dates, and places. → Check printed sources at libraries and depositories. → Use internet resources.

Verify compiled research by searching public records. → Locate residences on map. → Study area history and maps.

Study censuses. → Visit courthouses, cemeteries, and churches. → Add to charts. Cite sources. → File information systematically.

# 3
## technique

Use the following two steps to choose a type of record to search.

1. Considering the goal you have set, see Where Can I Find…? on page 27.

2. Make a list of records that may contain the information you are looking for to complete your goal. You need not search all of the records on the list, nor must you search in the order the records are listed. You may also skip records that you have already thoroughly reviewed.

*Courtesy of Connie Duran*

*Courtesy of Connie Duran*

# Where can I find certain facts?

After exhausting the personal knowledge and information you have in your home and within your immediate family, it is time to research outside your home. Following Step 2 of the Genealogy Research Cycle on page 23, it is time to choose a source of information. Different approaches and records are used depending on the information needed, the location where the family lived, and the time period. A secondary source may give a frame of reference from which to work, hopefully leading you to a primary source. Once you have set a goal to find a specific fact, decide which primary source would most likely have that information. Remember, information can be recorded in more than one place. If no primary sources are available, find two different secondary sources to be certain the information is accurate. (Refer to What are primary & secondary sources? on pages 18–19.)

# Where Can I Find...?

| If you need: | Primary sources: | Secondary sources: |
| --- | --- | --- |
| Birth date & place | church, vital, family Bible | military, census, cemetery, newspaper, obituary, tax |
| Death date & place | cemetery, church, military, probate, vital, family Bible | land, town, obituary |
| Maiden name | church, family Bible, land, military, probate, vital | census, compiled history, newspaper |
| Children's names & ages | church, family Bible, land, probate, vital | census, compiled history, immigration, obituary |
| Christening date & place | church, family Bible | journal |
| Marriage date & place | family Bible, marriage certificate | journal, newspaper |
| If divorced | court or divorce records, vital | journal, newspaper |
| Burial date & place | cemetery, death certificate | family Bible, family history |
| Where family lived | census, land, military, obituary | county history, newspaper |
| Family's religion | church, family Bible, cemetery | nationality |

Be aware that some normally considered primary sources may be secondary and vice versa. For example, if the mother is giving the date of birth for an obituary it is considered primary; whereas if the daughter was giving her mother's birth date, it is secondary information.

# 4
## technique

Use the following seven steps to prepare a research log.

1. Write the name of the person you plan to research and where he was living.

2. Write your name, address, and phone number on the page in case you lose it.

3. Write the "goal" objective information you are seeking. Keep the objective simple. By focusing on one question at a time, you will increase your chances for success.

4. As you research different documents, fill in the date you searched, cite the source, note what you were looking for, and what the results were.

5. Work on the same log page until the objective goal has been met to avoid duplicating researching of documents.

6. File the research log with the documents pertaining to the person whom you were researching to remind you where you have already looked for information.

7. When moving on to a new goal, fill out a new research log.

## How do I keep a research log?

As you locate and review different sources, it soon becomes impossible to remember every record you have searched and what you found or did not find. A Research Log, such as the one shown on page 29, tracks these details, keeping you or another family member from duplicating research.

As you review various documents and sources, write down which records you studied. Also list what you were looking for and the results of your search. You may need to return to a record when looking for different information. If you know "why" you looked at it the first time, you will not overlook the document, assuming you have already reviewed it.

Keeping a research log takes discipline. If you develop the habit at the beginning, it will become second nature. If you find nothing in a source, write "nothing located" and what you were looking for, then record the source so you do not research it again.

# Research Log

Ancestor's name _____

Research goal _____

| Search date | Record/call number | Source description author/title/year/page number | Comments | Results |
|---|---|---|---|---|
| | | | | |
| | | | | |
| | | | | |
| | | | | |
| | | | | |
| | | | | |
| | | | | |
| | | | | |
| | | | | |
| | | | | |
| | | | | |

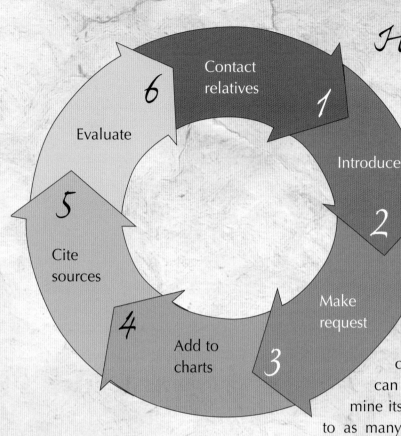

**Contact relatives** — 1
**Introduce** — 2
**Make request** — 3
**Add to charts** — 4
**Cite sources** — 5
**Evaluate** — 6

# 5

*technique*

Use the following six steps to obtain information from relatives.

1. Contact relatives.

2. Introduce yourself and explain why you are interested in the family.

3. Ask specifically for the information you want. Keep your request simple.

4. Add new information to charts.

5. Cite the information source, date, person, and how information was acquired.

6. Evaluate the information.

# How do I obtain information from my family?

Talk with as many relatives as possible to learn background information on or about your family. This can be done through personal visits, telephone calls, conventional letters, or e-mails.

Write down family stories you have heard and the sources of the stories as you remember them. Record as many names, places, and details as possible. Information handed down from generation to generation is considered oral history and cannot be used as documentation. However, it can lead you to the appropriate sources to determine its accuracy. When gathering oral histories, talk to as many older relatives as possible. This alone can produce 3–4 generations of an ancestry complete with siblings in each family, as well as spouses and children. If you have no older living relatives, older people in the community, especially those who lived near your family, may know a great deal about your family.

Prepare for an interview by making notes in advance about the questions you want to ask and by being familiar with the family members you are studying. When you talk with them, ask about more than facts and dates—get the stories of their youth and of the ancestors they remember. Try to phrase questions with "why," "how," and "what."

Take your time during the interview; do not quickly ask question after question—barely listening to the answers. The more enjoyable the interview is, the more relaxed and informative the person you are interviewing will be.

Ask about documents, pictures, or old papers relating to your family. If you have any of these items yourself, bring them along to share. It may jog their memories. Ask about personal data such as name spellings, religious affiliation, and family origins. From where did you or your family emigrate? Where are the places you have previously lived? Why did you move?

Immediately after the interview, transcribe your notes while everything is fresh in your mind. This is also a good time to note things you did not have time or forgot to ask, so you will be prepared for a follow-up interview. When interviewing the elderly, time is a factor if they are not in good health. Many may be burdened when reading through your notes and may require you or someone else to do that for them. If possible, schedule a second interview approximately two weeks after the first.

You might want to send a copy of your transcription to the person you interviewed and ask if there are any corrections or additions. Having them read the interview transcript may trigger additional memories.

When writing a letter, remember, most people do not easily sit down and write a long letter to address your questions. You may find it best to limit the number of questions. If your effort is successful, you can continue your correspondence with a few more questions each time.

When requesting information, enclose a self-addressed, stamped envelope for the reply. If there will be copying fees or other costs, be certain to send money.

If you are requesting information from actual documents rather than simply collecting facts, request a copy of the document for your files.

If during your correspondence you find that another family member is working on the same line you are, work together rather than duplicate work. Make assignments for each other and share your findings liberally.

Keep your findings well documented so when conflicting information arises you can make an accurate judgement on which facts may be true. Also be liberal with the information you collect with others who may be searching as well.

# 6

*technique*

Use the following four steps to fill out a pedigree chart.

1. The first individual name (1) is yours or the person whose ancestry is being done. Write the surname (last name) first in capital letters, then write the first (given) name and middle name followed by any necessary title. Use full names. Use the maiden name (surname at birth) of a woman rather than her married name.

2. List people as couples. Record the male on the top line and the female on the bottom. If you do not know the woman's maiden name, write her first and middle names, then leave a blank space to be filled in later. If there is a double or hyphenated surname, place the newer name last. If there is a nickname, include it in "quotes" after the given name. Underline any uncommon names or unusual spellings to indicate they are recorded accurately.

3. Information regarding birth, marriage, death, and burial dates are recorded underneath each relevant name. Use the European method of dating, with the day first, then the month, and then the full year. You may specify an approximate date as either "about" (abbreviated abt) or "circa" (abbreviated ca. or c.).

4. Record place names from smallest to largest (i.e. town, county/parish/district, state/province, country).

## What is a pedigree chart?

Genealogists organize family relationships and dates, using a Pedigree Chart such as the one shown on page 33. The chart is commonly referred to as a family "tree," with the extending lines acting as the "branches."

The pedigree chart serves as a master outline of your genealogy information. The chart not only shows how your family members relate to one another, but makes it easy to see what information you are lacking.

A pedigree chart only shows direct ancestors—there is not room for siblings, multiple marriages, cousins, aunts, and such. These relationships, however, are recorded on family group sheets. (See What is a family group sheet? on pages 36–37.)

There are a number of different presentations of charts. Though the pedigree chart shown is the most recognizable, the picture pedigree above, the Concept Chart on page 34, and the Fan Chart on page 35, all represent a broader range of information.

There will, no doubt, be blank spaces on a chart when you begin, and possibly even after years of research. Never assume or guess, as this will later be misconstrued as factual data. Avoid becoming discouraged. Each blank space represents a mystery for you to solve.

# Pedigree Chart

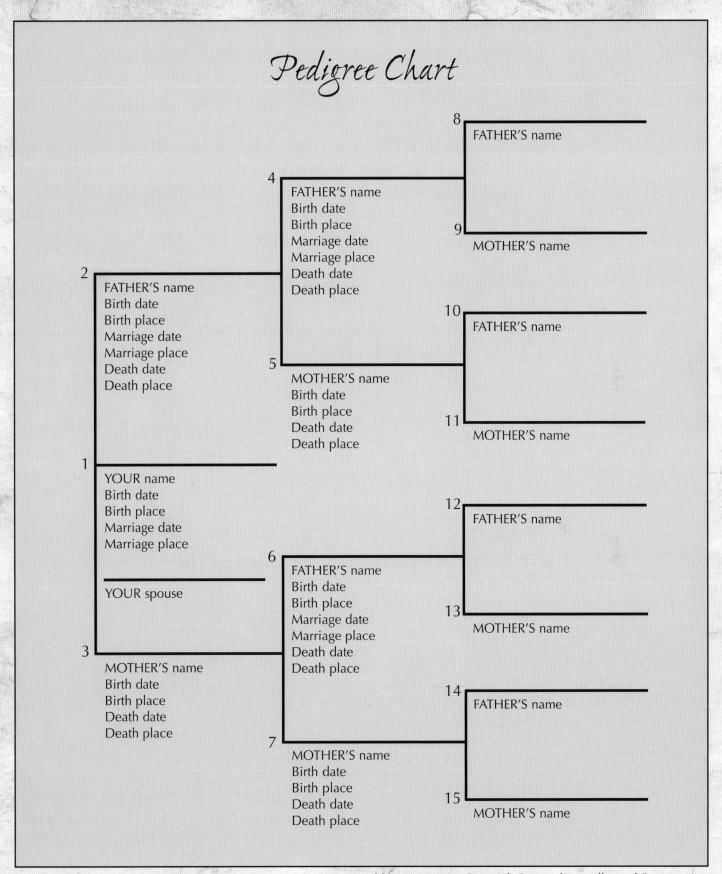

# Concept Chart

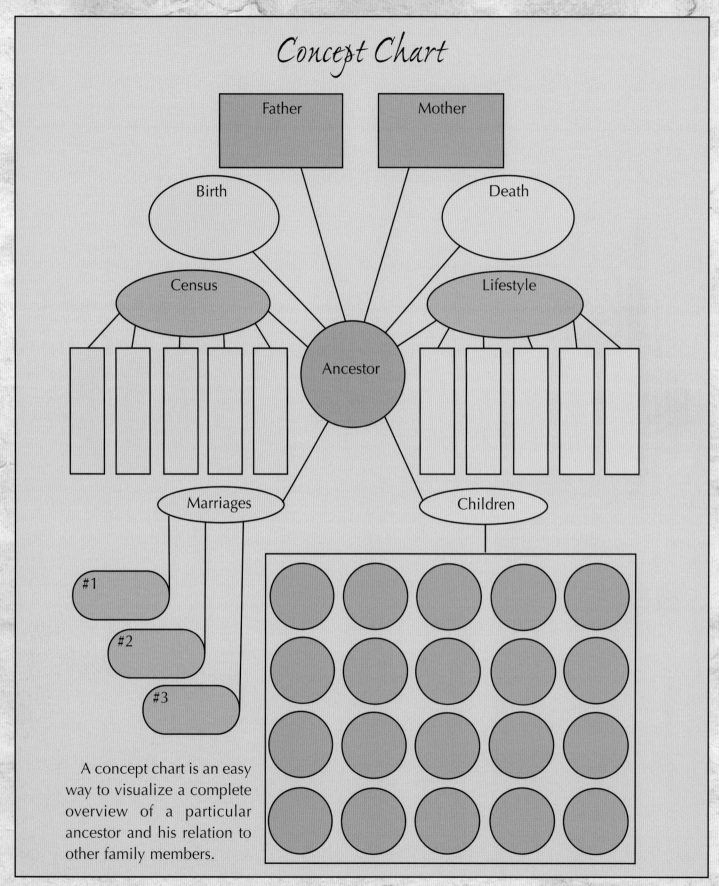

A concept chart is an easy way to visualize a complete overview of a particular ancestor and his relation to other family members.

# Fan Chart

A fan chart is an easy way to visualize a total ancestry. With four six-generation fan charts—one for each set of grandparents—placed together, this large circular chart shows the culmination of one's genealogy.

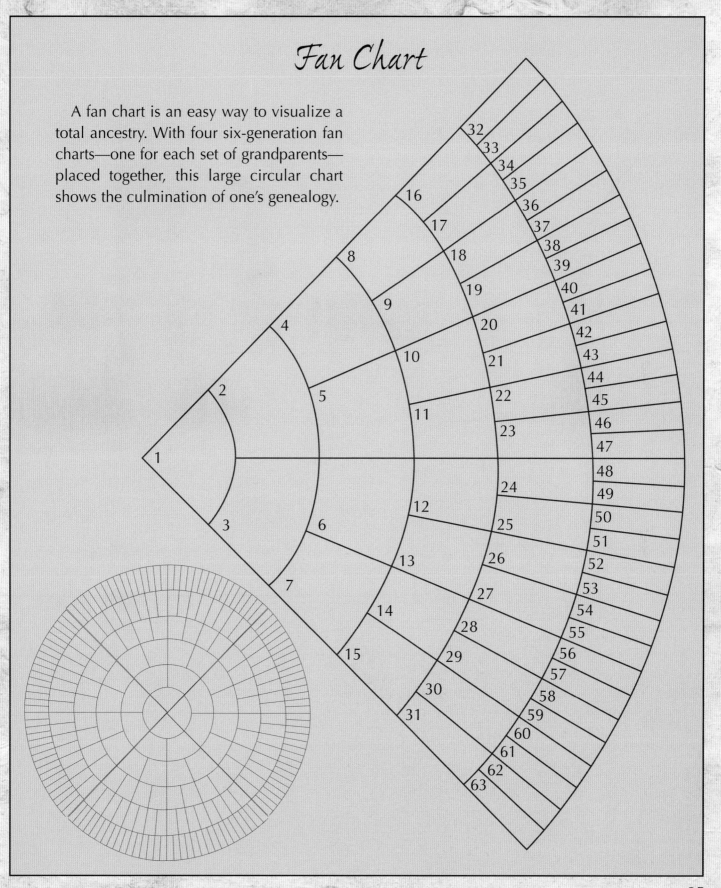

# 7
## technique

Use the following five steps to fill out a family group sheet.

1. Complete a Family Group Sheet, such as the one shown on page 37, for your immediate family. There are a variety of preprinted forms from which to choose.

2. Consistently record names, dates, and places. Place children in birth order. Do not forget children who died at birth or multiple births.

3. Make a separate family group sheet for every couple listed on your pedigree chart. If someone was remarried, start a separate family group sheet for that union. Make a family record for a couple with a child, even if they were never married. If a couple had no children, complete a chart showing such, so others will know this fact was checked and no issue was found.

4. Make family group sheets for aunts and uncles and their children as well, so as not to forget any cousins.

5. Cite your findings. (See How do I cite my sources? on pages 40–41.) Make notes of any pertinent information such as religion, occupation, or military service on the back of the family group sheet. Number these notes to create a source list. Use those numbers you have assigned to indicate exactly what pieces of information on your group sheet came from each source.

# What is a family group sheet?

While a pedigree chart identifies your ancestry and serves as a culmination of your work, the family group sheet, or record, is the tool to develop the pedigree chart.

The family group sheet lists the immediate family of a couple, whether they were married or not, including their children, parents, and any other spouses. A typical family group sheet has room to add data on collateral family lines and the information sources.

Anytime name spellings or questionable dates arise, such as three children all born on the same day but in different years, underline these notations so that others will know this information may look wrong, yet in fact is correct. This also goes for a child with a name typically different for its gender. The gender can be underlined, as well as the birth city if it is different than that of all the other children.

Do not be confused if more than one child had the same name. Early practice was to name children after older family members. If a child died young, the given name may have been given to another baby later. Do not confuse or discount the second baby, thinking it was the same as the first.

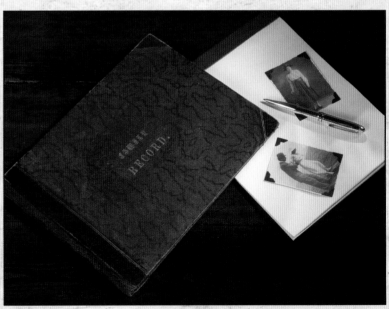

*Courtesy of Mary Flygare Gillette*

# Family Group Sheet

Husband_____ Occupation _____

Born_____ Place _____

Christened_____ Place _____

Married_____ Place _____

Died_____ Place _____

Father_____ Mother _____

Other Wives _____


Wife_____

Born_____ Place _____

Christened_____ Place _____

Died_____ Place _____

Father_____ Mother _____

Other Husbands _____

| Children List in birth order | Sex | When born When died | Where born Where died | Marriage date/place To whom |
|---|---|---|---|---|
| | | | | |
| | | | | |
| | | | | |
| | | | | |
| | | | | |
| | | | | |
| | | | | |
| | | | | |
| | | | | |

| Sources of information | Children's other marriages |
|---|---|
| | |
| | |
| | |

37

# 8
## technique

To analyze the records you find, ask yourself questions such as:
• What dates does this record provide?

• What places are given?

• Are the parents, children, or spouses named?

• What was the cause of death?

• What was the information source?

• Does the information from the record fit with what I already know?

• Were the witnesses at the event any relation to the family?

When choosing between two different document types, use the following guidelines to choose which facts to preserve:
• Use primary sources over secondary sources.

• Rely on original documents over a transcript of the document.

• Two independent sources are better than one source.

• Use actual dates over estimated.

• Use logical information over illogical.

• Use historically accurate information over historically inaccurate.

# How do I evaluate my findings?

Be accurate and alert when studying evidence and organizing facts into a logical order. Truth cannot be built on error or speculation. It is imperative that you extract from records only the facts actually there. Do not read into a record conclusions not justified by those facts. Just because a child is listed on the census as living in a household does not mean he is a child of the couple living there.

When researching a question, find all the records about the subject—not just the easy-to-find ones—then compare and analyze your findings. When discrepancies arise in names, places, dates, or relationships, compare the conflicting information and consider the sources.

Question the validity of the sources you uncover. Who gave the information in the document? Was the informant someone who knew the family well? It is often assumed that because the same statement appears in print in a number of books, it must be true because of the wealth of so-called evidence.

Keep in mind what you already know about the family. When did they live and where? Did they fight in a war? What were their occupations? Consider how major events may have affected these family members. (See the Historical Time-line Chart on pages 66–67.)

If you are not familiar with the place where a family event happened, learn about the history, geography, culture, language, and record depositories of the area to help you better understand the lifestyle, traditions, and activities of the people. Study basic historical events and practices of the people living at the time of your ancestors. This added knowledge will help you understand their actions, motives, and movements.

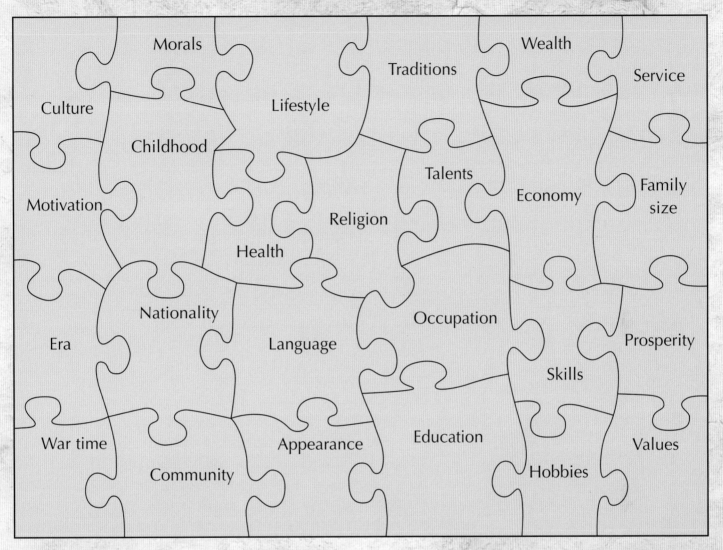

If you do not know the previous residence of an ancestor, read about the factors that caused migration to the area where you know they lived. Learn where other people came from and why they came. Step back from your research and look at the big picture.

Develop an interest in other people's genealogy to further your own knowledge of the people of the time or a location in that era. You may have success in finding that elusive place of previous residence if you follow a group of people backward in time instead of a single family.

Remember, the earlier the time period in which you are researching, the less consistent your ancestors were about the spelling of their surnames. Perhaps, some of them were illiterate and could not tell a record keeper how their names should be spelled.

Do not assume modern meanings for relationship terms. For example, in the 17th century, a stepchild was often called a "son-in-law" or "daughter-in-law," and a "cousin" could refer to almost any relative except a sibling or child.

Use as many records and refer to as much historical data as possible to piece together the lives and lifestyles of your ancestors.

When citing a source, obtain the following information:

**Book, family Bible, periodical:** title, year, author, publisher, page number

**Cemetery record:** cemetery name and location, grave site location

**Census record:** title, division, record location, form of record, page number

**Civil vital record/courthouse record:** record title, dates and numbers, location of document

**E-mail (printed on paper):** date sent, sender's name, recipient, e-mail address

**Land record:** title and type of record, government agency

**Letter:** sender, recipient, content, date

**Military record:** record title, file number, government agency, location of record

**Newspaper:** date, name & place of publication, page number, column number

**Oral interview:** interviewee, interviewer, date, location of record

**Photograph:** date taken, acquired from whom, identification of people

**Telephone:** date, caller's name, phone number, address, summary of data

**Tombstone:** name of deceased, cemetery name and location, date visited

**Web site:** description of information found, on-line address, date researched

## How do I cite my sources?

The importance of documentation in genealogical research cannot be stressed enough. It is not optional. When you find conflicting facts, you will want to be able to validate and choose which source is more accurate.

Question the validity of each source you uncover. Just because something is in print does not mean it is correct. Until you know differently, write down everything you find and the source until you can prove or disprove it.

Whether you are working alone, with other family members, or with a professional genealogist, it is imperative to know where you have already looked and what you have found. Otherwise they will be duplicating work you have already done. (Refer to How do I keep a research log? on pages 28–29.)

When citing information from a publication, photocopying the title page of the resource book or the periodical will avoid any copying errors. Also note the copyright information—usually found on the reverse of the title page—and the name of the depository on the photocopied paper. Transfer any relevant information to your records and file the backup copy in your files.

When taking notes, use high-quality paper and record information about only one family on a sheet of paper. Write the name of the family that the notes are about at the top of the page. Avoid recopying notes and citations; because every time you transcribe or copy something, you are introducing the possibility of a new set of errors. Make your original notes neat enough to use and proofread what you have written.

Record as much information as is known about the photographs and items you collect. Note the previous and current owners, what the article meant to the family, and when it was acquired. To avoid confusion, use full names, dates, and places when documenting.

The information collected about the photograph above was written on a piece of paper (right) and taped to the back. Avoid writing directly on the photograph.

*About 1905, Matilda Jane Martin Hennessey (seated in the chair) with 6 of her children, standing in front of their homestead home in Coke County, Texas. Due to the high temperatures, the bed on the porch was a permanent fixture. Photograph in possession of Tillie's granddaughter Barbara Hennessey Harvey.*

# 10
## *technique*

To organize and file your documents:
- Make a photocopy of original documents, before storing the original in an acid-free sheet protector.

- Label a manila folder with the names of your mother and father. Write their birth and death dates under their names. (See photograph below.) Make a similar folder for each set of grandparents and great-grandparents. Include alternate spellings if surnames have changed.

- Organize pedigree charts and family group sheets into a loose-leaf binder. (Refer to What is a pedigree chart? on pages 32–33 and What is a family group sheet? on pages 36–37.) Place a copy of the pedigree chart on the front of the notebook for easy viewing and to identify which relations are in the binder. (See photographs on page 43.)

- Use index tabs to divide the loose-leaf notebook into families. File each family group sheet by the husband's surname. Either file the most recent generation first or file the family group sheets alphabetically by surname.

- In each family section, place family group sheets, copies of vital records, census records, correspondence, research notes, and other materials as you acquire them. Keep an individual's documents with his parents' until he marries.

## How should I file my findings?

Devise a system that allows you to file your information quickly and easily. Do not become a slave to your filing method. If you are spending more than a few moments rummaging through stacks of paper to find something, then your system is not working. Order and organization bring success and completion to your work.

As your research continues, you will add more folders and loose-leaf binders for additional families. Also, as you gather maps, census records, and family stories, more folders will be necessary to hold these documents.

If your research takes you onto another pedigree chart, add another loose-leaf binder to your collection. Place the pedigree chart for the families included on the front of the binder.

Carry this "working" notebook with you to oral interviews, the library, the cemetery, and such while researching, as a quick reference of information. Be certain your name, phone number, and address are written in your notebook in the event it is lost.

Since genealogy evolves around family relationships, your files and research findings should be shared with interested relatives, preserved, and passed down to the next generation.

Keeping your notes and filing system clearly labeled will assist others when they refer to your research information. It is important that others benefit from your findings so that their work does not duplicate yours. Passing on your compiled information and research, ties families together.

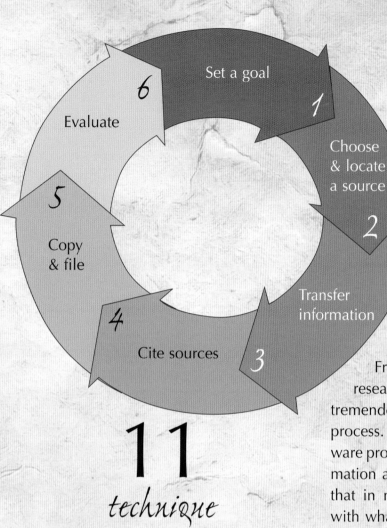

Set a goal

6

Evaluate

1

Choose
& locate
a source

5

Copy
& file

2

4

Transfer
information

Cite sources

3

# 11
## technique

If you are using a computer now rather than handwriting your information, do not skip the six basic steps of research.

1. Set a goal.

2. Choose and locate a source containing the information you are seeking.

3. Transfer the information directly into your computer program, following the software's instructions.

4. Cite your sources.

5. Print a hard copy of your record and file with your other records.

6. Evaluate data to see if the goal was met.

## How can a computer help my research?

From organizing and matching families to researching over the internet, computers have made a tremendous advancement in the family researching process. With more than 40 different family-history software programs available, these programs store vital information and link individuals together into families. With that in mind, genealogists should become acquainted with what a computer can and cannot do, then decide what is appropriate for their research needs. It is worth the expense in both time and money to learn about computers and how they can benefit research. Because new genealogical software programs regularly come onto the market, and those already in use are constantly being upgraded, it would be inappropriate to endorse any particular computer products here. However, a few sample pages are shown on page 45.

To learn more about the new computer software products available, subscribe to a genealogy specialty publication or participate in a computer-interest group associated with genealogical societies. You may also want to consult with other family members on what they prefer. It may benefit you to buy the same type of software that they use since you will be trading information back and forth with them.

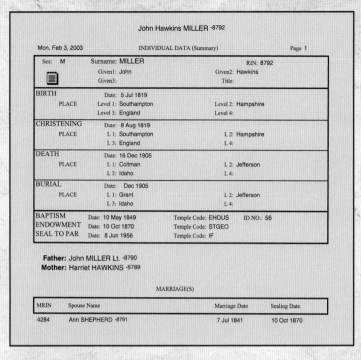

**John Hawkins MILLER -8792**

Mon, Feb 3, 2003      INDIVIDUAL DATA (Summary)      Page 1

| Sex: M | Surname: MILLER | | RIN: 8792 |
|---|---|---|---|
| | Given1: John | Given2: Hawkins | |
| | Given3: | Title: | |

**BIRTH**
Date: 5 Jul 1819
PLACE Level 1: Southampton    Level 2: Hampshire
Level 3: England    Level 4:

**CHRISTENING**
Date: 8 Aug 1819
PLACE L 1: Southampton    L 2: Hampshire
L 3: England    L 4:

**DEATH**
Date: 16 Dec 1905
PLACE L 1: Coltman    L 2: Jefferson
L 3: Idaho    L 4:

**BURIAL**
Date: Dec 1905
PLACE L 1: Grant    L 2: Jefferson
L 3: Idaho    L 4:

| BAPTISM | Date: 10 May 1849 | Temple Code: EHOUS | ID NO.: 56 |
| ENDOWMENT | Date: 10 Oct 1870 | Temple Code: STGEO | |
| SEAL TO PAR | Date: 8 Jun 1956 | Temple Code: IF | |

**Father:** John MILLER Lt. -8790
**Mother:** Harriet HAWKINS -8789

MARRIAGE(S)

| MRIN | Spouse Name | Marriage Date | Sealing Date |
|---|---|---|---|
| 4284 | Ann SHEPHERD -8791 | 7 Jul 1841 | 10 Oct 1870 |

Word processing has saved researchers countless hours of transcribing original records and organizing materials. Electronic scanning allows text, illustrations, and photographs to be reproduced in almost any format.

Do not rely solely on your computer. Be certain to have a printed copy of your work and back-up your files often. Do not skip the steps of researching the validity of records because they are so easy to collect in your computer.

**Family Group Record**

Mon, Feb 3, 2003      Page 1

**Husband:** John Hawkins MILLER

| | | |
|---|---|---|
| Born: | 5 Jul 1819 | Place: Southampton, Hampshire, England |
| Chr.: | 8 Aug 1819 | Place: Southampton, Hampshire, England |
| Died: | 16 Dec 1905 | Place: Coltman, Jefferson, Idaho |
| Bur.: | Dec 1905 | Place: Grant, Jefferson, Idaho |
| Marr: | 7 Jul 1841 | Place: Southampton, Hampshire, England |

**Father:** John MILLER Lt.    **Mother:** Harriet HAWKINS

**Wife:** Ann SHEPHERD

| | | |
|---|---|---|
| Born: | 8 May 1825 | Place: Deptford, Kent, England |
| Chr.: | 29 May 1825 | Place: Saint Nicholas, Deptford, London, England |
| Died: | 27 Mar 1910 | Place: Coltman, Jefferson, Idaho |
| Bur.: | 1910 | Place: Grant, Jefferson, Idaho |

**Father:** Nathaniel John SHEPHERD    **Mother:** Mary ANDREWS

Sex Children    List each child (living or dead)
M/F    in order of birth

1. Name: Harriet Hawkins MILLER    Spouse:
F Born: 28 Jul 1843   Place: Southampton, Hampshire, England
Chr.:   Place:
Died: 15 Jul 1844   Place:
Bur.:   Place:
Marr.:   Place:

2. Name: Alice Ophelia MILLER    Spouse: Mathew William DALTON
F Born: 19 Jul 1845   Place: Southampton, Hampshire, England
Chr.:   Place:
Died: 13 Jan 1900   Place: Provo, Utah, Utah
Bur.: 17 Jan 1900   Place: Willard, Boxelder, Utah
Marr.: 5 Sep 1868(div)   Place: Salt Lake City, Salt Lake, Utah

3. Name: John Shepherd MILLER    Spouse: Elizabeth Campbell HODGE
M Born: 12 Mar 1848   Place: Southampton, Hampshire, England
Chr.:   Place:
Died: 6 Jul 1907   Place: Grant, Jefferson, Idaho
Bur.:   Place: Grant, Jefferson, Idaho
Marr.: 10 Oct 1870   Place: Salt Lake City, Salt Lake, Utah

4. Name:    Spouse:
Born:   Place:
Chr.:   Place:
Died:   Place:
Bur.:   Place:
Marr.:   Place:

5. Name:    Spouse:
Born:   Place:
Chr.:   Place:
Died:   Place:
Bur.:   Place:
Marr.:   Place:

Name and Address of Submitter:

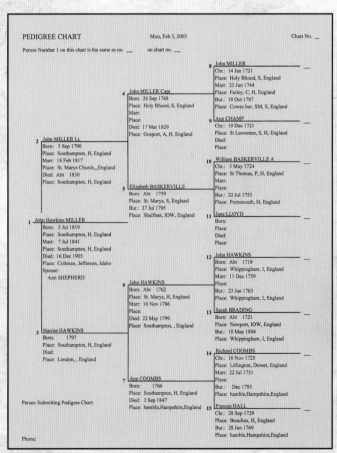

**PEDIGREE CHART**    Mon, Feb 3, 2003    Chart No. __

Person Number 1 on this chart is the same as no. __ on chart no. __

8 **John MILLER**
Chr.: 14 Jan 1721
Place: Holy Rhood, S, England
Marr: 23 Jun 1744
Place: Farley, C, H, England
Bur.: 18 Oct 1787
Place: Cowes bur, SM, S, England

4 **John MILLER Capt**
Born: 26 Sep 1748
Place: Holy Rhood, S, England
Marr:
Place:
Died: 17 Mar 1829
Place: Gosport, A, H, England

9 **Ann CHAMP**
Chr.: 19 Dec 1721
Place: St Lawrence, S, H, England
Died:
Place:

2 **John MILLER Lt.**
Born: 5 Sep 1790
Place: Southampton, H, England
Marr: 18 Feb 1817
Place: St. Marys Church,,,England
Died: Abt 1830
Place: Southampton, H, England

10 **William BASKERVILLE A**
Chr.: 3 May 1724
Place: St Thomas, P, H, England
Marr:
Place:
Bur.: 22 Jul 1755
Place: Portsmouth, H, England

5 **Elizabeth BASKERVILLE**
Born: Abt 1759
Place: St. Marys, S, England
Bur.: 27 Jul 1795
Place: Shalfleet, IOW, England

11 **Jane LLOYD**
Born:
Place:
Died:
Place:

1 **John Hawkins MILLER**
Born: 5 Jul 1819
Place: Southampton, H, England
Marr: 7 Jul 1841
Place: Southampton, H, England
Died: 16 Dec 1905
Place: Coltman, Jefferson, Idaho
Spouse:
Ann SHEPHERD

12 **John HAWKINS**
Born: Abt 1719
Place: Whippingham, I, England
Marr: 11 Dec 1759
Place:
Bur.: 23 Jan 1763
Place: Whippingham, I, England

6 **John HAWKINS**
Born: Abt 1762
Place: St. Marys, H, England
Marr: 16 Nov 1786
Place:
Died: 22 May 1799
Place: Southampton, , England

13 **Sarah BRADING**
Born: Abt 1721
Place: Newport, IOW, England
Bur.: 10 May 1804
Place: Whippingham, I, England

3 **Harriet HAWKINS**
Born: 1797
Place: Southampton, H, England
Died:
Place: London, , England

14 **Richard COOMBS**
Chr.: 16 Nov 1725
Place: Lillington, Dorset, England
Marr: 22 Jul 1751
Place:
Bur.: Dec 1793
Place: hamble, Hampshire, England

7 **Ann COOMBS**
Born: 1766
Place: Southampton, H, England
Died: 3 Sep 1847
Place: hamble, Hampshire, England

15 **Frances HALL**
Chr.: 28 Sep 1729
Place: Beaulieu, H, England
Bur.: 28 Jun 1769
Place: hamble, Hampshire, England

Person Submitting Pedigree Chart:

Phone:

*Examples of forms from the Personal Ancestral File® software program*
*Reprinted by permission. Copyright©1995 by Intellectual Reserve, Inc.*

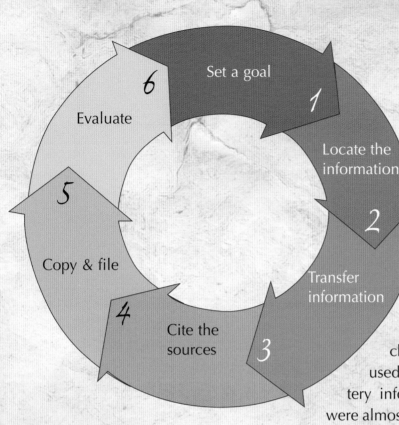

Set a goal

6 Evaluate

1 Locate the information

5 Copy & file

2 Transfer information

4 Cite the sources

3

# 12
*technique*

Use the following six steps to help you find information about your ancestor on the internet.

1. Set a goal.

2. Find the information on-line.

3. Transfer information to your records.

4. Cite the source.

5. Make a hard copy to keep in your files.

6. Evaluate data to see if the goal was met.

## How can the internet help my research?

The introduction of the internet significantly changed the accessibility to myriad records used in researching. Courthouse records, cemetery information and military data to some people were almost unobtainable. Though an abundance of data is available, it is important to understand that several key sources of information must be researched in other places before turning to the internet. Building a good foundation before you go on-line will help you verify the facts you discover on-line.

Be aware that most of the resources widely available on the internet are secondary or compiled sources. (Refer to What are primary and secondary sources? on pages 18–19.) Only a few sites offer access to images of original materials. Compiled sources vary in their degree of accuracy and completeness. Treat information found on-line as any other secondary source. Just because it is on the internet does not mean it is correct. Carefully cite the source from which you received it. (Refer to How do I cite my sources? on pages 40–41.) Evaluate every new source of information and reevaluate every conclusion. (Refer to How do I evaluate my findings? on pages 38–39.)

One of the biggest temptations in computer genealogy is the acquisition of "instant ancestors." When you find a distant cousin working on your family lines and that person has placed a wealth of material onto a genealogy

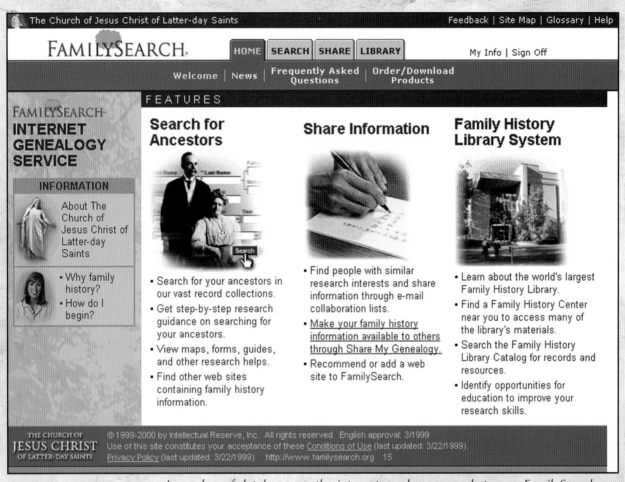

*A number of databases on the internet can be accessed at www.FamilySearch.org*
*Reprinted by permission. Copyright©1999–2002 by Intellectual Reserve, Inc.*

database, it is a simple matter to transfer the information to your database. However, check the validity before adding this material to your records. If you choose to add selected portions to your family group sheets, be certain you cite the source from which you took them, not the sources cited by the person who gave the information to you. If on the other hand, you can use their information to obtain the original sources and examine them yourself, then cite the original sources.

Like any other research, keep a research log of where you have looked on-line to avoid duplicating your research. (Refer to How do I keep a research log? on pages 28–29.)

The best place to begin your search on-line is at a comprehensive genealogical site, which may lead you to other sites of interest to your research. The publications of enormous databases of census records, vital records, military records, and cemetery records are available—some through government agencies others through private vendors. Depending upon the site, there may be a charge to access the material. A few of the most popular sites are listed on page 110.

*Family History Library, Salt Lake City, Utah*
*Reprinted by permission. Copyright©1999 by Intellectual Reserve, Inc.*

# 13
## technique

Use the following six steps to help find information in the Family History Library.

1. Set a goal.

2. Check the FamilySearch file on-line.

3. Check automated databases.

4. Check the family history collection.

5. Add newly acquired information to your records and cite your sources.

6. Evaluate data to see if the goal was met.

# What can I find in the Family History Library?

The two libraries with the most comprehensive collections of local histories and historical documents are the Family History Library in Salt Lake City, Utah, and the Library of Congress in Washington, DC. (See What can I find in the Library of Congress? on page 51.)

The Family History Library was founded in 1894 to gather genealogical records and to assist members of The Church of Jesus Christ of Latter-day Saints (Mormons) with their family history and genealogical research.

Today, this is the largest library of its kind in the world. The records found in the library are not exclusive to the members of the Church. The library is open to the general public at no charge and accommodates over 2,000 patrons each day.

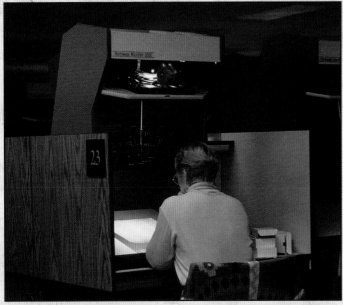

*Patron using a microfilm reader*
*Reprinted by permission.*
*Copyright©1999 by Intellectual Reserve, Inc.*

From immigration records to military records to compiled family histories, a wide variety of historical records have been secured from around the world and are made available within this library.

Patrons have access to microfiche and microfilm readers to preview the over 2.2 million rolls of microfilmed genealogical records and 742,000 microfiche records. Printed materials include 300,000 books and serials, and 4,500 periodicals.

At the library, patrons have access to computers which link to a number of large databases. The database FamilySearch includes several files:

• The Ancestral File—contains approximately 35.6 million names that are linked into families.

• The International Genealogical Index—contains approximately 600 million individual names with an addendum containing 125 million names.

• The Family History Library Catalog—lists the more than two million titles in the Family History Library, and serves both as an index to the library and as a catalog to other book collections, including books at the Library of Congress.

• The Social Security Death Index—provides information for millions of deceased persons who had social security numbers and whose deaths were reported to the Social Security Administration.

• The Military Index—lists 100,000 US military personnel who died in Korea and Vietnam.

With records from the United States, Canada, the British Isles, Europe, Latin America, Asia, and Africa, the Library's collection concentrates on records of deceased persons living before 1920.

Also available are more than eight million paper records of families, arranged alphabetically by surname and over 70,000 books containing printed family histories and biographies.

For researchers not within the vicinity of the Genealogy Library, The Church of Jesus Christ of Latter-day Saints makes these records available at locations across the United States in satellite units called Family History Centers. (See What is a Family History Center? on page 50.)

*Extensive microfiche collections*
*Reprinted by permission.*
*Copyright©1999 by Intellectual Reserve, Inc.*

# 14

## technique

Use the following six steps when working at a Family History Center.

1. Set a goal.

2. Check the FamilySearch file on-line.

3. Check automated databases.

4. Check the family histories.

5. Add the appropriate names, dates, places, and notes to your records.

6. Evaluate to see if the goal was met.

# What is a Family History Center?

For those unable to visit the Family History Library in Salt Lake City, The Church of Jesus Christ of Latter-day Saints has developed 3,400 branches of this library throughout the world called Family History Centers. At these locations patrons have access to computers and the same internet databases as at the Family History Library.

The centers are staffed with trained volunteers. All Family History Centers are open to the public and anyone is welcome to use them without charge.

Patrons may order records, microfilm, and microfiche from the library in Salt Lake City to be sent to their local Family History Center. Some centers have materials unique to their locality which do not circulate to other Family History Centers or the Family History Library.

With the accessibility of so many documents and records through the Family History Library and Family History Centers, no longer is it necessary to travel to countless courthouses and cemeteries to find information.

# 15

## technique

Use the following six steps when working at the Library of Congress.

1. Set a goal.

2. Check the Library of Congress index on-line.

3. Check automated databases.

4. Check the family histories.

5. Add the appropriate names, dates, places, and notes to your records.

6. Evaluate to see if the goal was met.

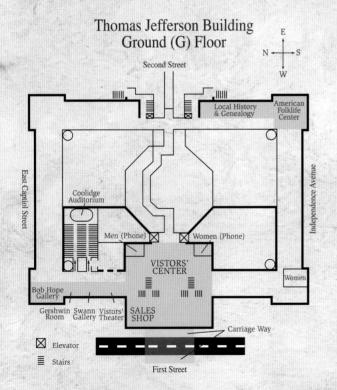

Thomas Jefferson Building
Ground (G) Floor

# What can I find in the Library of Congress?

The Library of Congress, located in Washington DC, is the nation's oldest federal cultural institution and the largest library in the world. It contains more than 120 million items on approximately 530 miles of bookshelves. The collections include more than 18 million books, 2.5 million recordings, 12 million photographs, 4.5 million maps, and 54 million manuscripts.

The Local History and Genealogy Reading Room, located at the Library of Congress in the Thomas Jefferson Building, is also one of the leading genealogical collections in the country. It shelves more than 40,000 genealogies and 100,000 local histories. Patrons have access to collections of manuscripts, microfilms, newspapers, photographs, maps, and published material, as well as 10,000 indexes, guides, and other reference works.

FamilySearch, the CD-ROM computer system of the Family History Library, is available for use at three workstations in the Local History and Genealogy Reading Room.

The Library of Congress web site hosts a list of other internet sources on local history and genealogy, such as genealogical libraries and genealogical, archival, and historical resources.

*John Geddes Miller with parents John Shepherd & Elizabeth Hodge Miller*

## Section 3:
## Beyond the basics

# 16
## *technique*

When verifying facts, check as many records as possible in the following order:

• Family records. (Refer to What information do I already have? on pages 14–17 and see What can I find in a family Bible? on pages 58–59.)

• Compiled sources and the internet. (See What are compiled sources? on pages 56–57. Refer to How can the internet help my research? on pages 46–47.)

• Census records which may lead to immigration or naturalization records. (See How do I use census records? on pages 60–61, How can I use immigration records & passenger lists? on pages 86–87, and How can I use naturalization & citizenship records? on pages 88–89.)

• Vital records. (Refer to What are primary & secondary sources? on pages 18–19. See What information can I find in cemeteries? on pages 72–73 and What information can I find in church records? on pages 74–75.)

• Government records, including probate, court, tax, and land records. (See What can I learn from land records? on pages 76–77, What can I learn from tax records? on pages 78–79, and What can I learn from wills & probate records? on pages 82–83.)

• Military records. (See What can I learn from military records? on pages 80–81.)

## What is a chain of evidence?

The building of a pedigree chart is comparable to the links in a chain. The chain depends upon each link to add strength by the amount of evidence obtained. In research, the goal should be to build up a chain of evidence in which each link is strong enough to support the next. Each link should be connected with the one before by as much "connecting link" evidence as is possible, to make the connection as strong as possible. (See the Flowchart of Research Steps on page 55.)

Search as many records as possible to verify the information you collect. The lack of connecting evidence often means that pedigrees are built on circumstantial evidence alone. One "missing link" or "weak link" may subsequently lead your research into the wrong family.

Certainly family stories and traditions have a place. Every piece of information concerning an ancestor is valuable to lead you in the direction of primary sources. (Refer to What are primary & secondary sources? on pages 18–19.) This does not mean, however, that every story is correct. Research and document family traditions. Write a detailed account of a tradition as it is currently understood. Find and evaluate primary sources, then record the story accurately along with how you proved or disproved it. (Refer to How do I evaluate my findings? on pages 38–39.)

# Flowchart of Research Steps

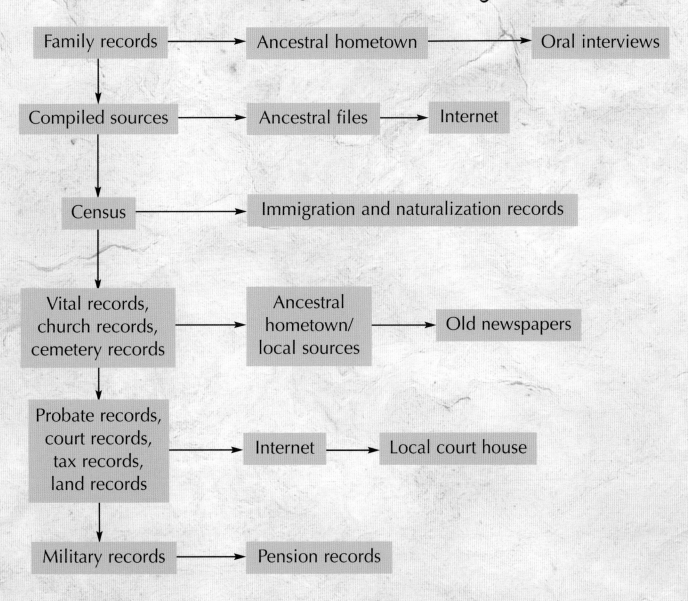

Family records → Ancestral hometown → Oral interviews

Compiled sources → Ancestral files → Internet

Census → Immigration and naturalization records

Vital records, church records, cemetery records → Ancestral hometown/ local sources → Old newspapers

Probate records, court records, tax records, land records → Internet → Local court house

Military records → Pension records

cemetery census will compiled sources

military records court records land records tax records

# What are compiled sources?

Thousands of brief biographical sketches have been collected and published in compiled biographies. These collections most often include biographies of early settlers and prominent or well-known citizens of a particular state, county, or town. Other books feature biographies of scientists, writers, artists, or other vocations.

Compiled sources are an essential part of the early phase of gathering family history. Though they are secondary sources and not always accurate, they provide a framework upon which to add data collected from other sources. Do not assume that because someone else has done work gathering family history that the information in it is totally accurate and complete. Names, places, dates, and relationships should be verified whenever possible by using primary sources such as vital or church records or two independent sources.

Be thorough, but reasonable. If in spot-checking previously researched work you find that it is accurate, you do not have to redo all the work. Be consistent and logical when reviewing compiled facts. Were the children in a family born less than nine months apart? Were they born

# 17
## technique

Use the following six steps to help you find information about your ancestor in previously done research.

1. Ask your relatives if you can copy the genealogical information they have. (Refer to How do I obtain information from my family? on pages 30–31.) Make copies of these items.

2. Using a search engine, check the internet for relevant automated databases. (Refer to How can the internet help my research? on pages 46–47.)

3. Find family histories or biographies.

4. Make photocopies of the information you find for your file.

5. Add the appropriate names, dates, places, and notes to your pedigree charts and family group sheets.

6. Evaluate the accuracy of the information you found.

out of normal childbearing years of the mother? Were two children given the same name while both were still living? Do any dates conflict? If so, recheck the information.

As you gather information, do not assume everyone with the same last name was related. Recording everything about everyone with the same surname will cause confusion later. Before introducing people into your records be certain they truly belong.

A collection of compiled sources in the form of published family histories can be found in the Family History Library. (Refer to What I can find in the Family History Library? on pages 48–49), on genealogical web sites (Refer to How can the internet help my research? on pages 46–47), or at public archives and libraries.

Remember that book indexes rarely include the names of all persons mentioned in the book. If it appears that a book is likely to have valuable information, spend some time skimming its contents for your ancestor's name.

Search libraries first for published records and manuscript collections. In some cases, archival facilities may contain many of the same types of materials as libraries.

# 18
## technique

Use the following five steps to help you find information about your ancestor in a family Bible.

1. Locate the family Bible for your family. You will need to talk with other members of your family to find if there is one in existence and its whereabouts.

2. Photocopy the family records page and the title page. If it is too fragile, you may have to transcribe this information.

3. Check for loose papers inserted in the Bible—you may find obituary clippings, or funeral memorial cards. Do not remove them from their original place— they may mark favorite or meaningful Bible passages. Extract any pertinent information from the saved treasures within the Bible.

4. When citing a source, make notes on who currently is in possession of the Bible and who the former owners were.

5. Evaluate the information written in the Bible. Compare the written dates with the publication date of the Bible to conclude if the information and dates were recorded at the time of the event or years later.

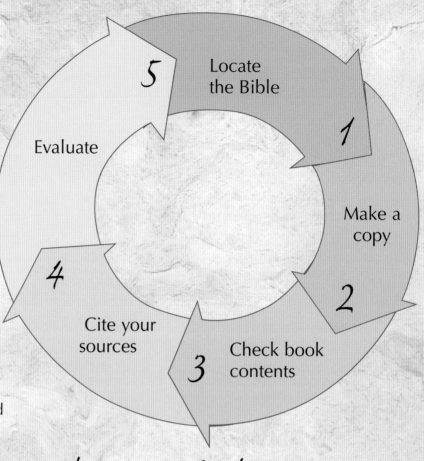

## What can I find in a family Bible?

In years past, the family Bible was the place where family records were kept. The amount of information you can gather from this source will vary. Written family records differ widely as to trustworthiness. When entries were made in family Bibles immediately after each event occurred, they are usually very accurate and such records rank with the best that can be obtained. However, many people did not begin keeping a Bible record until several years after a marriage, and entered the births of their older children and their parents from memory.

Keep the Bible away from the natural elements and protected. If you want to display the book, keep it under glass to protect it from light, dust, and people.

*Courtesy of Margaret Fisher Ostlund*

# 19
## technique

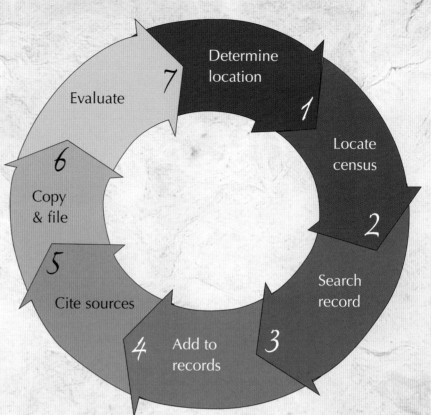

Use the following seven steps to help you find information about your ancestor in a census record.

1. Get a general idea of where your family was living during a census-record period of time. This will determine which censuses you will search.

2. Start with the last census taken during the life of your ancestor. Determine and locate a census.

3. Search the census records, working backward until you have searched all of the censuses taken during the life span of your ancestor. If you skip a census, you may miss additional information needed to help you identify the complete family unit or earlier generations. To track the information gathered from each census, keep a log of your findings. (See the Census Research Log on page 63.)

4. Add the information to your records.

5. Cite your sources.

6. Make a copy of each census as well as the page before and after in the event family members are living nearby. File the copies with your records.

7. Evaluate data to see if the goal was met.

## How do I use census records?

Census records are one of the most valuable primary sources created by the federal government. Federal censuses have been taken every 10 years since 1790. Some states have state censuses, and a few even have county censuses.

Each census offers slightly different information depending on what Congress was interested in recording at that time. The earlier federal census records name only the head of household in each locality and number of males and females in different age categories. Later censuses include the name of every member of the household and their relationship to the head of household, the address, birth dates, location of parents' birth, the number of years married, date of immigration, occupation, and value of personal and real estates.

Do not assume the relationships between those living in the house. Sometimes a person in a household is listed as a "boarder," but is actually a relative; or the woman in the house is the head-of-household's sister rather than spouse and still has the same last name. Check marriage, deed, and probate records to connect the people in the household.

Tracing a family through the census provides a migration history and the locations in which research should be centered. As with all genealogical research, census records should be used from the present, moving backward. Many things happen in a 10-year period of any family.

Enumerators visited each family in their districts and asked a set of specific questions. Those questions and the format in which they are recorded varied throughout history. People are listed in census records in enumeration order, grouped by county and state. Information was taken from house to house, neighbor to neighbor, down the streets and roads.

*Martha Porter and children with U.S census enumerator Orderville, Utah, 1910*

*Melancthon & Jane Hodge Jones with family, Kansas,1892*

61

Notice who your families' neighbors were. Families seldom moved alone; they moved in groups related by blood, marriage, religion, ethnic origins, and social status. People tended to marry within their own social and economic groups.

Families with the same surname as the one you are researching will be of particular interest. Look for similarities of unusual first names and coincidental places of birth.

If you do not find the family you are seeking in an index, look for those allied and associated families you have been recording as you do your research. Just because a person is not listed in an index does not mean he was not in the original record, but you may find him or his movements through an associated family. Go directly to the census film where the associated family is listed and search the county where you think they should have been living to see if they are nearby.

Unfortunately, census records are prone to a variety of errors. Perhaps a neighbor supplied the names and ages of the family members. Even if the enumerator received correct information, he may have written it incorrectly. He was working from the spoken word, translating it to paper. The copyist may have made errors. Record the information just as you find it—make no effort to "correct" the record. Cite your source. Then check information that may be inaccurate with other records.

County and state boundaries changed over time and, since that is how census records are filed, be aware of these changes. If you cannot locate your ancestors from one census to the next, check surrounding counties. Your ancestor may have lived in one place, but boundary changes list him in census records of a different county.

*Henry Edward & Lillie Adams Hennessey family migrating from Texas to Arizona, September, 1911*

# Census Research Log

| | |
|---|---|
| Ancestor's name | |
| Birth date/place | |
| Parents' names | |
| Marriage date/place | |
| Death date/place | |
| *1800* | |
| *1810* | |
| *1820* | |
| *1830* | |
| *1840* | |
| *1850* | |
| *1860* | |
| *1870* | |
| *1880* | |
| *1890* | |

# 20
## technique

### How can I use maps for researching?

To help picture in your mind the movement of your ancestors, mark a map of where your ancestors traveled and lived. Choose a map depending on their travel patterns. If they traveled extensively, a map of the United States may be appropriate; whereas if they jumped around in a local area, a state map may give you more detail.

• Depending on the map you choose, mark the county, township, or location of your ancestor's residence.

• Make copies of your maps and file with other information for each family.

• If possible secure historically accurate maps of your ancestor's time—these are especially helpful when boundaries and city names changed.

Maps can help you visualize the geographic location, terrain, and living conditions experienced by your ancestors. Libraries and archives have collections of maps, while commercial firms sell reproductions of historical maps. Different map types will supply you with a variety of information to study. Topographic maps show natural contours of the land. Mountains were a barrier to early travel. Waterways were also barriers, but served as a means of travel. This knowledge may help you find the way your family traveled from place to place.

Soil maps may help with emigration information. Your ancestors knew how to grow particular crops, and when they emigrated to a new area, they looked for a region similar to their old home in terms of terrain, soil, and vegetation. The agricultural schedules of the census will help you learn what crops your ancestors grew.

Using a map when working with census records is imperative. Since the information is collected through the county and town limits, it would be hard to visualize and find your family without a map of their current times.

*The Henry Edward & Lillie Adams Hennessey family migrating from Texas to Arizona, September, 1911*

Creating a generational migration map, such as the one below, gives an overview of your ancestors' movements. It is interesting to see how far apart your ancestors started. At some point their paths crossed, their families met, and their children married. In some instances, these newly allied families traveled together. It is also interesting to see the correlation between your ancestors movements and the historical events of the day. (See the Historical Time-line Chart on pages 66–67.) Compare where you live now in relation to where your ancestors chose to settle.

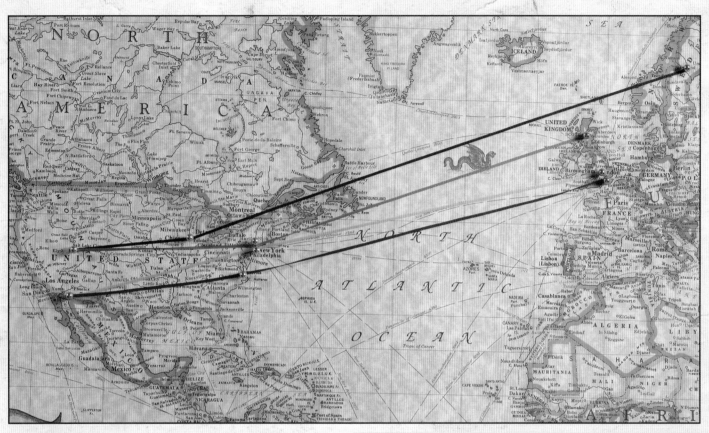

## Family key:

### Nils Christian Flygare
1841—Born in Sweden
1876—Traveled from Sweden to Chicago
      Led wagon train to Ogden, Utah

### John Hawkins Miller
1819—Born in Southampton, England
1866—Sailed to the United States
      Took oxen team to Salt Lake City, Utah

*Note: For purposes of instruction, some information about the families above has been modified.*

### William Standifird
1687—Born in England
1707—Settled in Maryland
1771—His grandson Ephraim moved to
      Kentucky
1868—His great-grandson John moved to
      Bountiful, Utah
1878—John settled Snowflake, Arizona

### Thomas Hennessey
1856—Born in England
1870—Stowed away on a ship from England
1872—Appeared in Mason County, Texas
1916—Moved to Holbrook, Arizona

# Historical Time-line Chart

(example 1800–1950)

Family name _____

| 1800 | | 1825 | | 1850 | |
|---|---|---|---|---|---|

Timeline entries (listed left to right):

- 1801–1809—Thomas Jefferson was president
- 1803—Louisiana Purchase
- 1803—Ohio became a state
- 1812—Louisiana became a state
- 1812–1815—War with Britain
- 1816—Indiana became a state
- 1817—Mississippi became a state
- 1817–1825—James Monroe was president
- 1818—Illinois became a state
- 1819—Alabama became a state
- 1820—Maine became a state
- 1821—Missouri became a state
- 1836—Arkansas became a state
- 1836–1845—Republic of Texas was formed
- 1837—Michigan became a state
- 1840—Oregon Trail used
- 1845—Texas & Florida became states
- 1846—Great Irish potato famine began
- 1846—Iowa became a state
- 1846–1848—War with Mexico
- 1847—Mormon pioneers in Salt Lake valley
- 1848—Wisconsin became a state
- 1849—California gold rush began
- 1850—California became a state
- 1858—Minnesota became a state
- 1858—Colorado gold rush began
- 1859—Oregon became a state
- 1860—Pony Express service began
- 1861—Kansas became a state
- 1861–1865—Civil War
- 1864—Nevada became a state
- 1865—Slavery abolished
- 1867—Nebraska became a state
- 1869—First transcontinental railroad completed

When piecing together an ancestor's life, work chronologically. Using land, (See What can I learn from land records? on pages 76–77), census (Refer to How do I use census records? on pages 60–61), and tax records (See What can I learn from tax records? on pages 78–79) compile a simple chronological idea of where the generations of your family lived. Using the Historical Time-line

| 1875 | | 1900 | | 1925 | | 1950 |

Timeline events:

- 1876—Colorado became a state
- 1876—Bell patented the telephone
- 1877—Edison invented the phonograph
- 1879—Edison invented the lightbulb
- 1886—State of Liberty dedicated
- 1889—Washington, Montana, South Dakota & North Dakota became states
- 1890—Idaho & Wyoming became states
- 1892—Ellis Island opened to immigrants
- 1894—Edison introduced motion pictures
- 1898–1899—Spanish–American War
- 1903—Wright Brothers' first flight
- 1908—Henry Ford introduced Model T
- 1911—Mexican Revolution
- 1912—Arizona became a state
- 1912—New Mexico became a state
- 1912—Titanic sank
- 1914—First national income tax
- 1917–1918—US involvement in WWI
- 1920—Women's right to vote
- 1920—Popularity of the radio increased
- 1923—First talking movies
- 1927—Charles Lindbergh soloed the Atlantic
- 1928—Penicillin discovered
- 1929—Great Depression began
- 1933—Prohibition ended
- 1934—"Dust Bowl" drought
- 1935—Social Security Act
- 1936—Spanish (Spain) civil war
- 1937—Hindenburg exploded
- 1940—Churchill became prime minister
- 1941–1945—US involvement in WWII
- 1944—Ballpoint pen introduced
- 1950–1953—Korean War

Chart above or a similar chart, keep track of the movements of your family members.

In the appropriate boxes of a chart, list where your ancestors were living and what they were doing at a certain time in history. Be aware of what was happening historically. This may put your ancestors' movements into perspective and give reasons why they moved when they did.

# 21
## *technique*

To protect documents and photographs:

• Avoid touching originals. Turn pages with a pencil eraser or a rubber finger.

• Make a photocopy of the original. Make copies from the copy.

• Write facts about a photograph on a sheet of paper and secure it to the back. Do not write directly on the photograph.

• Keep negatives in a separate envelope from the photographs.

• Place original documents in previously labeled sheet protectors. Do not write directly on the documents.

• Store documents in steel file cabinets or in acid-free storage boxes.

# How can photographs help my research?

Most vintage family photographs are tucked away in the closets, drawers, and scrapbooks of older family members. These treasures should be found, preserved, copied, and shared with other family members. Ask parents, aunts and uncles, grandparents, cousins, etc., if they have family photographs. If so, offer to make copies of them for other family members and have the originals preserved before returning them.

Local museums or libraries may have photographs of previous area residents. Some local county historical societies may have photographs of prominent 19th century citizens who may also be members of your family.

*Robert G. Taylor, 1955*

George T. Hennessey, 1925

George T. and George D. Hennessey, 1935

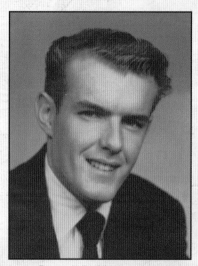

George D. Hennessey, 1951

Genealogy becomes more than just collecting dates and names when a picture is found. Photographs put a face to a name, while showing the living conditions, attire, expressions, and geographic area of the time.

When collecting and studying family photographs it is not uncommon to see personal and physical traits that have been carried through the generations, giving a sense of belonging. The photograph above is of father and son. These same two men are pictured above (right) in their late teens and show a number of similar facial features.

The men pictured at right are of the same family. This cherished photograph of grandfather, grandson, and two great-grandsons was taken days before the grandfather passed away.

George D., Steve, Ed, Bob Hennessey, 1962

69

# 22
## technique

Use the following seven steps to help you find your family information in cemetery records.

1. Choose an ancestor to locate.

2. Determine the town he probably died in by searching a town index of cemetery records in the Family History Library Catalog. (Refer to What can I find in the Family History Library? on pages 48–49.)

3. Obtain the record book or film.

4. Locate your ancestor in the record.

5. Make a photocopy of the record.

6. Cite your sources, including the name of the library, archive, etc.

7. Evaluate data to see if the goal was met.

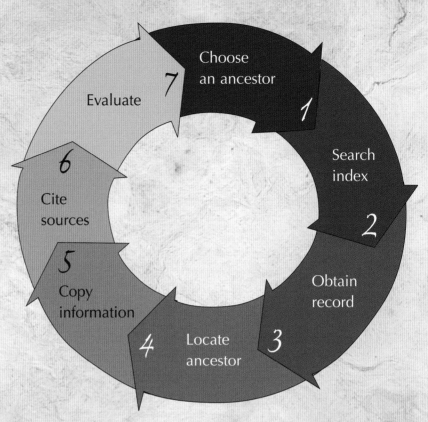

*City Cemetery, Draper, Utah, est. 1854*

# What are the differences in cemeteries?

There are a variety of graveyards. Large cemeteries are well maintained and records are kept about each plot. If a large cemetery is still in use, you may locate the sexton or caretaker and inquire about records.

Smaller cemeteries may be full of unmarked graves and worn tombstones. Such old, weathered tombstones are notoriously difficult to read. In these cemeteries, the sexton may do everything from digging the graves to keeping the records. Likely, the cemetery records will be at his home. If he has lived in the town for a long time, he may be a valuable resource to you as he will probably know quite a bit about your family's history.

Sexton's records may include burial registers, plots, and deeds. They will also tell you if more than one person is buried in the same lot (common if a mother and infant die in childbirth or if twins die together) or if a body has ever been exhumed and moved to another cemetery or plot.

You may discover the names of ancestors buried in the cemetery without a marker.

If the cemetery where your family members are buried is next to a church, there may be records about the burial among the church's records.

Some families established burial grounds on their farms, which may be located far from the road. If the farm is no longer owned by the family, the burial ground may have fallen into neglect. The stones may have fallen over and the cemetery may have virtually disappeared.

Occasionally, cemetery records and tombstones never existed. Some mountain people refused commercial funerals. They buried their own dead, with neighbors helping to prepare the body for burial, until well into the mid-twentieth century.

Some cemeteries are literally moved when public work projects, such as dams or highways have the right-of-way. These cemetery records may be in the library, with the historical society, or in the home of the sexton.

Cemetery names change. An 80-year-old newspaper obituary may say an ancestor was buried in a seemingly nonexistent cemetery, when in reality the name was changed when a second cemetery was started in the same town.

*St. Andrew Church, Hampshire, England, built in 1100 A.D.*

# 23
## technique

Use the following six steps to help you find family information in cemeteries.

1. Determine the cemetery in which your ancestor is buried.

2. Using a plat map or walking the cemetery, locate your relative.

3. Transcribe the information off the tombstone. Be certain to look at markers nearby for other family members.

4. Cite your sources.

5. File this relative's new information with your notes.

6. Evaluate data to see if the goal was met.

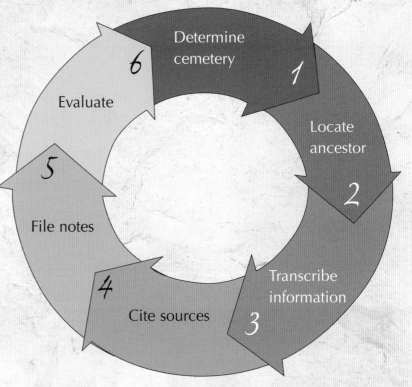

1 Determine cemetery
2 Locate ancestor
3 Transcribe information
4 Cite sources
5 File notes
6 Evaluate

## What information can I find in cemeteries?

Visits to family cemeteries will give you a great deal of information. Visiting a cemetery on Memorial Day may give you a chance to meet distant family members who have come to remember your common ancestors.

Once you locate your ancestor, write down the facts listed on the tombstone. This may include birth, marriage, and death information as well as the names of spouse and any children. Be certain to check both sides of the stone. Write down information of stones close to your relative, especially those with the same surname. These names may be a clue to children that you were not aware of who died young or women not recorded in other family and government documents. Notice any marks of military service or fraternal organizations, which may suggest other records to check.

When visiting a cemetery make notes which will allow you to easily find ancestral plots on any return visit or direct other family members to their locations.

A large cemetery may already have a plat map showing the cemetery grid layout, such as the map below. For small cemeteries, draw your own diagram of how the cemetery is situated. Label the graves not only of your family members, but also of people buried in adjoining plots. This will help you locate the area again and may give additional information of family members to whom you did not previously know you were related.

You may also choose to photograph tombstones such as the stone at right. Write the cemetery name and location on a piece of paper and attach to the back of the photograph, along with the date you took the picture.

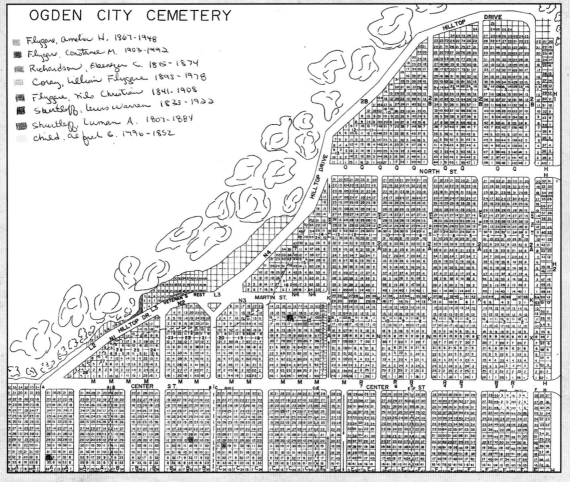

# 24
## technique

Use the following seven steps to help you locate and use church records.

1. Set a goal.

2. Identify where your ancestor was living. Determine which denomination your ancestor attended during that time.

3. Find and search the records of your ancestor's church.

4. Make a copy of the information. Some choose to take a photograph of fragile records when a copy cannot be made.

5. Transfer information onto your records.

6. Cite your sources.

7. Evaluate data to see if the goal was met.

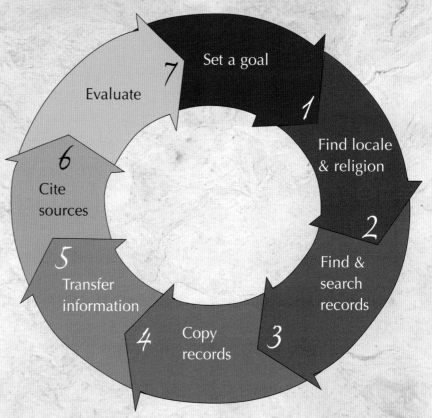

# What information can I find in church records?

Your ancestor probably attended a church in a town where the family lived. Records kept by churches are generally referred to as church or parish records. The locations of these records vary between states and between denominations. When searching for church records, start with the church closest to the recorded event then move out to neighboring churches.

In numerous communities, there was no established church. Meetings were held whenever a minister was in town. In other communities, there were numerous denominations—some were funded by the town and included in town records. Organized religion was not the rule, although Quakers, Protestant Episcopal Church, and Mormons were among the more conscientious in keeping church records. These records may be at a central depository of that particular religion. Check with libraries and archives of the religion favored by your ancestor.

Be aware that church records are among the most difficult to locate. Usually maintained by the minister and housed at his home or at the church, they often were victim to moisture, rodents, insects, or time. Some records became lost when ministers moved and took the records with them. Other records may have been preserved and are kept in a central location.

Besides being a major source of vital-record materials, church records may indicate migration patterns, since groups of people commonly traveled together. They may also provide insight to the values and intrigues of a community.

Church records generally contain information on christenings, baptisms, marriages, and burials. Though each denomination is different in its practices and methods of record keeping, you may also find names, dates, relationships, and where the parents lived. There are certain events which are only recorded through a church affiliation, such as infant baptisms, illegitimate children vital records, blacks—both free and slave, membership records including baptism date; date of removal such as death, excommunication, or transfer of membership; and the calling of a particular minister.

When reviewing church records, be aware of the names of witnesses and bondsmen, since they were often relatives or close friends.

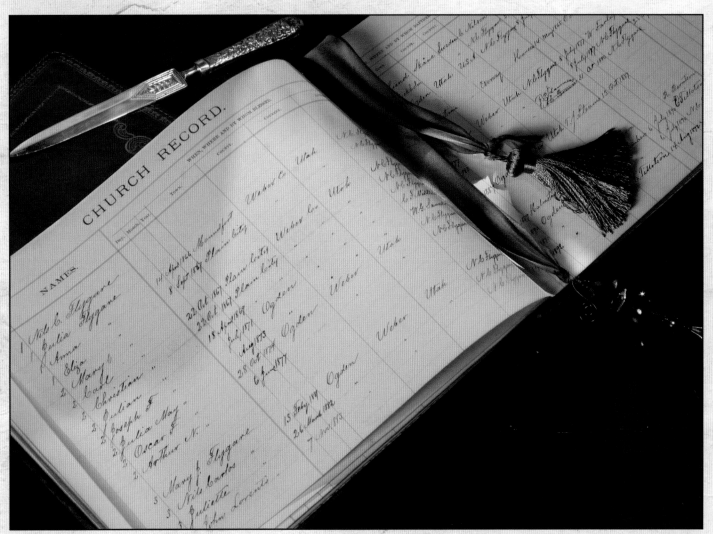

*Courtesy of Mary Flygare Gillette*

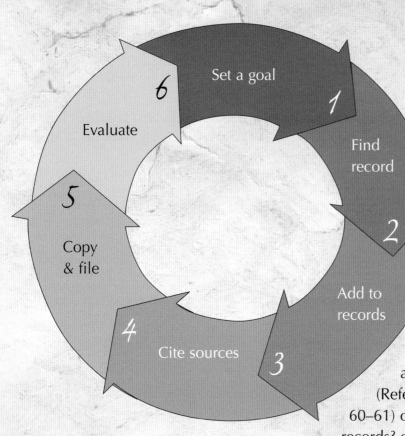

Set a goal

6

Find record

Evaluate

1

5

2

Copy & file

Add to records

4

Cite sources

3

# 25
## technique

Use the following six steps to help you find information in land records.

1. Set a goal.

2. Choose a location. Find the relevant land records.

3. Add the information to your records.

4. Cite your sources.

5. Make copies and file with your records.

6. Evaluate data to see if the goal was met.

## What can I learn from land records?

Land was a measure of success among ancestors—the more you owned, the more successful you were. The promise of land was usually the motivation for emigration to a new country or to move west. To determine if an ancestor owned land, check census records (Refer to How do I use census records? on pages 60–61) or tax records (See What can I learn from tax records? on pages 78–79.) Since 90 percent of the free males in the United States in 1850 owned land, land records are the most plentiful sources of genealogical information for this time period.

Land records track the migration patterns of ancestors, especially prior to the 1790 census. Besides helping to pinpoint a person to a specific location in a time frame, land records often listed where your ancestor lived before purchasing this land and the names of his spouse, children, grandchildren, parents, or siblings.

Deeds are the legal documents that transfer title of real property from one party to another. Usually the first acquisition of a piece of land was from the government, either state or federal, and those documents conveying title are called grants or patents. They are often recorded in county deed books.

The seller or grantor of a parcel of land wrote a deed conveying title to the buyer or grantee, such as the one shown on page 77. The legal document was presented to the proper clerk of the county where the land was located and it was copied into record books.

# In the Name of the State of Texas.

No. 567

## To all to whom these Presents shall come, know ye.

I, R B Hubbard      **Governor of the State** aforesaid, by virtue of the power vested in me by Law, and in accordance with the Laws of said State, in such case made and provided, do, by these presents, Grant to Wm W Martin his heirs or assigns, Forever, One hundred and Sixty (160) Acres of Land, situated and described as follows:

In Mason County Known as Sur No 801. on the waters of Katemcy creek about 12 ¾ miles N 17° W from Mason by virtue of his affidavit Made before the Clerk of the County Court for Mason County May 26th 1877 Under. An Act for the benefit of Actual Occupants of the Public Land. approved May 26th 1873.
Beginning At a Stak for S W cor No 759. N E Cor of No 743 + S E Cor of this Sur. a P.O. 20" brs S 10½ W 47 Vs. a P. O. 12" brs. S 20½" W 51 Vs Thence N 950 Vs a Stk for S W Cor a L O 10" brs. S 84 W 57 Vs a P.O. 6" brs N 68½ Vs   Thence N 950 Vs a Stk. for N W cor. a L O 8" brs N 81½ W 9¾ Vs. P.O. 10" brs. S 63½ E 45 Vs   Thence E 950 Vs. a Stak for N E Cor. a P.O. 8" brs S 81½ E 2 Vs. a B P. 14" brs N 48½ E 15 Vs   Thence with W line of No 759 South 950 Vs. to the beginning
Bearings mkd ⧻

File 852
Bexar

Hereby relinquishing to him the said Wm W Martin and his heirs or assigns Forever, all the right and title in and to said Land, heretofore held and possessed by the said State, and I do hereby issue this Letter Patent for the same.

**In Testimony Whereof,** I have caused the Seal of the State to be affixed, as well as the Seal of the General Land Office.

Done at the City of Austin, on the Twenty sixth day of January in the year of our Lord one thousand eight hundred and Seventy Eight

J J Groos    **Commissioner of the Gl. Land Office.**      **Governor.**   R. B. Hubbard

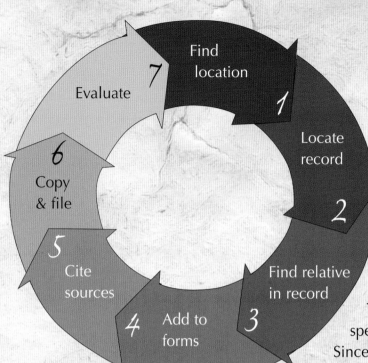

Evaluate

7 Find location

6 Copy & file

1 Locate record

5 Cite sources

2

4 Add to forms

3 Find relative in record

## 26
### *technique*

Use the following seven steps to help you find information about your ancestor in tax records.

1. Learn where your ancestor was living during the time frame you are researching.

2. Locate the tax records for that area and during that time.

3. Find your relative in the tax record.

4. Add information to your forms.

5. Cite your sources.

6. Make a copy and file in your records.

7. Evaluate data to see if the goal was met.

## *What can I learn from tax records?*

Using tax records can track the movements of your ancestors. They are among the earliest records available in the United States. In the absence of other records, tax records are vital. They place your ancestor in a specific place at a specific time and reflect his economic status.

Since tax records are compiled each year, it is best to use them in a series instead of one at a time. It is possible to track how long an ancestor lived in a particular area by where he appears in the tax records. Establish when he first appears in the records, then follow his name through the tax lists every year until you find the last year his name appears. When his name disappears, it means he either moved, died, or became blind or poor.

*Flygare chicken farm, Afton, Wyoming*

| OWNER | LANDS | | | TOWN LOTS | | | HORSES | | CATTLE | | MULES | | SHEEP | | Household and Kitchen Furniture | Money on hand or at Interest | Merchandise | Miscellaneous Property | TOTAL VA[LUE] |
|---|---|---|---|---|---|---|---|---|---|---|---|---|---|---|---|---|---|---|---|
| | Abst. No. | ORIGINAL GRANTEE | No. of Acres | Value | No. of Lot | No. of Block | Value | CITY or TOWN | No. | Value | No. | Value | No. | Value | No. | Value | | | | | |
| Crowell Wm. Hy. | | | 502 | 502 00 | | | | | 1 | 40 00 | 200 | 500 00 | | | | | | | | 139 0 |
| Jno. H. Crowell Adm'r (Taylor Smith) | | | | | | | | | | | | | | | | | | | | |
| Cunihan T. J. | | | 400 | 570 00 | | | 3 44 | 1000 00 | Brownwd. Tx. | 5 | 200 00 | 100 | 400 00 | | | | | | | | 600 |
| Crowell D. C. No. 52 | | J. B. Bennett | 440 | 440 00 | 209 | 400 00 | | do. | | | | | | | | | | | | | |
| 89 Leroy Forrester | | | | | 6 | 5A 50 00 | | do. | | | | | | | | | | | 1800 00 25 00 | 5490 0 |
| Clark, James | | | | | | | | | 16 | 400 00 | 400 | 1600 00 | | | 43 | 45 00 | | | | | 1880 |
| Cain, D. D. | | | | | | | | | 2 | 80 00 | 400 | 1600 00 | 2,200 00 | | 4 | 4 00 | | | 60 00 | | 36 67 |
| Caster N. G. | | | | | | | | | 4 | 200 00 | 902 | 340 00 | | | | | | | 5 00 | | 195 |
| Cap. John | | | | | | | | | 2 | 150 00 | 2 | 40 00 | | | | | | | 40 00 | | 110 |
| Clemens, Mary Jake | | | | | | | | | | | | 14 | 40 00 | | | | | | | |
| | | | | | | | | | 2 | 50 00 | 4 | 150 00 | | | 38 00 | | | | 38 00 | | 143 |
| Chandler W. H. | | | | | | | | | 6 | 240 00 | 405 | 330 00 | | | | | | | 30 00 | | 600 |
| Cox H. P. | | | | | | | | | | | 2 | 40 00 | | | | | | | | | 40 0 |
| Coffell L. H. | | | | | | | | | 4 | 120 00 | 29 | 245 00 | | | | | | | 40 00 | | 403 |
| Clark Ja. L. | | | | | | | | | 2 | 100 00 | | | | | | | | | | | 100 |
| Coler D. T. | | | | | | | | | | | | | | | | | | | | | |
| Case H. G. | | | | | | | | | 6 | 240 00 | 405 | 1350 00 | | | 33 | 66 00 | | 1000 00 | 150 00 | | 2930 |
| Case, James | | | | | | | | | 2 | 100 00 | 24 | 240 00 | | | | | | | 10 00 | | 550 |
| Chandler Jane | | | | | | | | | 3 | 120 00 | 300 | 1500 00 | | | 6 | 18 00 | | | | | 1890 |
| Chandler Abbot | | | | | | | | | 5 | 150 00 | 100 | 50 00 | | | 20 | 30 00 | | | 30 00 | | 710 |
| Chandler John | | | | | | | | | 2 | 150 00 | 200 | 200 00 | | | 13 | 10 00 | | | | | 560 |
| Chester D. L. 141 | 555 | W. G. Blair | 160 | 160 00 | | | | | 9 | 360 00 | 20 | 100 00 | | | 65 | 130 00 | | | | | 77 |
| Clark Bay. | | | | | | | | | 2 | 150 00 | | | | | 60 | 60 00 | | | 2 00 | | 2 0 |
| Crowell H. W. | | | | | | | | | 5 | 250 00 | 10 | 50 00 | | | 20 | 40 00 | | | | | 3 0 |
| Curtis H. G. | | | | | | | | | 2 | 800 | | | | | | | | | | | 80 |

1873 Brown County, Texas tax record

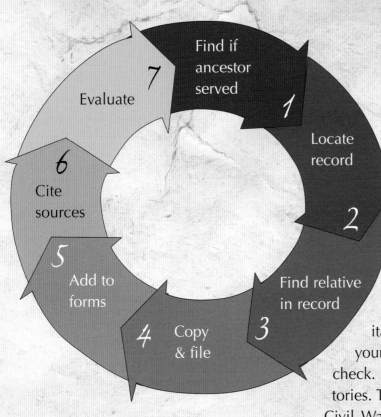

Find if ancestor served

Locate record

Evaluate

Cite sources

Add to forms

Copy & file

Find relative in record

7

6

5

4

3

2

1

**27**

*technique*

Use the following seven steps to help you find information about your ancestor in military records.

1. Learn whether or not your ancestor served in a war and in which branch.

2. Locate the military record.

3. Locate your relative in the military record.

4. Add information to your forms.

5. Make a copy of the record and file information with your records.

6. Cite your source.

7. Evaluate data to see if the goal was met.

# What can I learn from military records?

As you research your ancestors back through time, consider their participation in wars. (Refer to the Historical Time-line Chart on pages 66–67.) If you find that your ancestor may have been involved in a war, search for military records. If you do not know whether or not your ancestor served, there are a number of places to check. Review obituaries, tombstones, or compiled histories. The 1910 federal census identifies veterans of the Civil War. The Military Index on www.FamilySearch.org lists 100,000 US servicemen who served in the Korean War or the Vietnam War. (Refer to How can the internet help my research? on pages 46–47.)

Military service often creates two types of records: service records and pension records. Military service records for people who served in the armed forces in the last 75 years are protected by privacy laws. Military records for most American soldiers are held at the national level. The National Archives in Washington, DC, have records of soldiers from the Revolutionary War through the Spanish–American War (1898), including those for Confederate service in the Civil War.

Service records provide the unit your ancestor served in, which may lead to other military records. Limited information can be found including whether he enlisted or was drafted, the discharge date, pay records, and whether any injuries were sustained.

Pension records are among the richest military records, containing birth date and birth place, marriage facts, residence following the war, and sometimes information about children and other family members. Pension records of the Revolutionary and Civil Wars and subsequent wars contain a wealth of information on the soldier and his family. Usually, you need to know the state from which he served and the branch of service. Ex–Confederate soldiers applied for pensions from the state governments according to their state of residence. While the pensions were administered at the state level, payments to veterans and their widows were often made through county offices, generating local records.

American soldiers were either regulars or volunteers. Regular soldiers are what we think of today as career military service people. Volunteer soldiers, even those who were drafted, are citizens called upon for service in times of war. The records for regular soldiers are filed separately from those of volunteers.

Besides military service records, soldiers generated records when applying for benefits. During

*Horace Richardson, 1897–1955*
*Fought in two world wars*

the Civil War, some state governments passed laws to care for widows, and children of servicemen. These lists may be found in courthouses.

Soldiers who served in wars before the Civil War applied for bounty land under the various laws passed by Congress. Records about the land they received were generated at the county level when they recorded their land acquisitions.

The National Archives in Washington, DC, are the largest depository of military records in the United States. (Refer to What can I find in the Library of Congress? on page 51.) An entire microfilm catalog is devoted to military records. Copies of those microfilm publications are available at major libraries with genealogical collections. Military records can also be found at the Family History Library. (Refer to What can I find in the Family History Library? on pages 48–49.)

*1863 disability discharge*
*Courtesy Georgia Department of Archives and History*

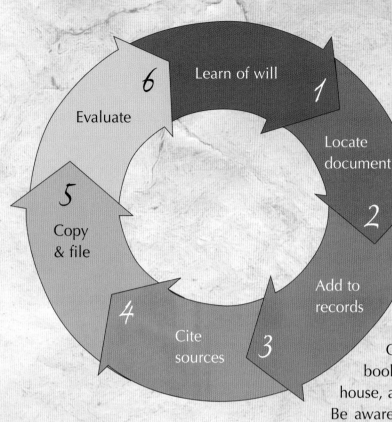

6 Evaluate

1 Learn of will

2 Locate document

3 Add to records

4 Cite sources

5 Copy & file

# 28
## technique

Use the following six steps to help you find information about your family in wills and probate records.

1. Learn if your ancestor left a will.

2. Locate any will or probate records—normally these are found in the records of the county in which he passed away.

3. Add information to your forms.

4. Cite your sources.

5. Make a copy of the record and file the information with your records.

6. Evaluate data to see if the goal was met.

## What can I learn from wills & probate records?

The process of submitting a will to the proper legal authorities is known as probate. Once proved, the will is transcribed into a will book. These books are kept in the county courthouse, and each one usually has its own index.

Be aware that wills are not always filed immediately after the individual's death. If a record is not found, search the years following the person's death.

When you find the probate packet for one of your ancestors, photocopy each paper. Study the papers in the packet to find important clues about this family. It is also important to locate the will in the will book and copy it.

Probate records are any court records created after an individual's death that relate to the court's decisions regarding the distribution of his estate, such as inventories, distributions of estates, letters of administration, sales of estates, and inquest documents.

On these records you may find the individual's death date, the names of family members, family relationships, and residences. You may also learn about the adoption or guardianship of minor children and dependents.

While probate records are one of the most accurate sources of genealogical evidence, they must be used with some caution. They may omit the names of deceased family members or those who had previously received an inheritance, or the spouse mentioned in a will may not be the parent of the children mentioned. Be careful of the terms that imply relationships, e.g. sister, cousin, senior, infant. Sister, for example, may refer to a female of the same religious faith or to a sister-in-law, and not to an actual sibling.

When extracting information, be certain to list everyone mentioned. Write the names exactly as they appear. Include references to relationships.

Note any provisions for orphaned children, mention of children's religion, or references to apprenticeship. Record the date of the will and the date that the will was probated in court.

When you cite the will, include the county, state, book, and page number. Note if it is the original will or a clerk's transcribed copy.

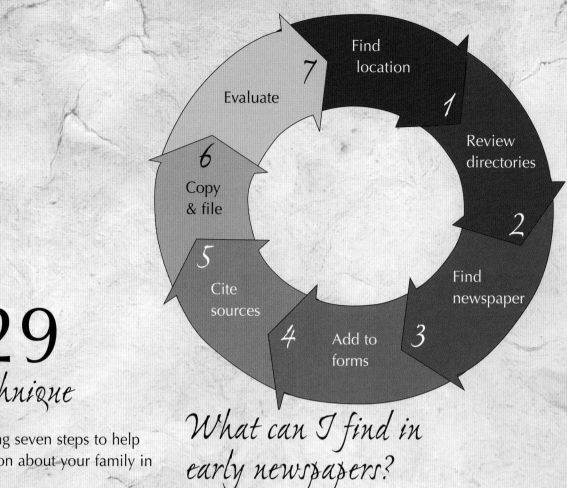

The following circular diagram labels (clockwise from top):

1. Find location
2. Review directories
3. Find newspaper
4. Add to forms
5. Cite sources
6. Copy & file
7. Evaluate

# 29
## technique

Use the following seven steps to help you find information about your family in early newspapers.

1. Learn where your ancestors lived.

2. Check the local library for the *Gale Directory of Published and Broadcasting Media* to find newspapers currently in print and information about their predecessors. Also check *Ayer Directory of Publications* for information about newspapers that are out of print.

3. Find newspapers in the location and time period of your ancestors.

4. Add the new information to your forms.

5. Cite your sources.

6. Make a copy of the record and file it with your records.

7. Evaluate data to see if the goal was met.

## What can I find in early newspapers?

Before television and radio, newspapers played an important role in the lives of people. They were filled with news and genealogical information. Though many of such newspapers are no longer in print, back issues are often available on microfilm. Newspaper collections may be located in state libraries, local libraries, or newspaper offices. Many 19th century newspapers have been indexed. Some of the state historical societies have produced guides to newspapers.

Early newspapers have a different look than today. Events were often combined into one story that ran for several columns with no heading to indicate the change of topic. Some newspapers reported weekly news from one particular town or another under a special heading. News traveled slowly in the past, so check a few days after an event occurred.

Early newspapers give a wealth of both historical and

Nelda L. Riniker, Edward B. Flygare
Recite Vows in Jackson Church Rites

personal information. It is common to find in a newspaper: birth or marriage announcements, death notices, court summons or citations, estate notices, unclaimed mail at the post office, general interest news that may include names of families moving west or visiting from out of town, church news that included baptisms and confirmations, or separation and divorce notices.

Obituaries are one of the greatest treasures. They are often filled with information. They may list maiden names, church and cemetery locations, marriage dates, occupations, military service, political offices, and even the names of family members who had died previously.

# Florence REMINDER
## AND
# BLADE-TRIBUNE

VOL. 91    FLORENCE, ARIZONA 85232    THURSDAY, FEBRUARY 8, 1973    NUMBER 6

## Retired Prison Guard Perishes in Flames

(PHOTO BY FRANK CONRAD)

Henry Edward Hennessey, 97, died early Sunday morning when flames engulfed his frame home near Christiansen Road and Arizona Hwy. 287.

Pinal County Sheriff's deputies said that Mr. Hennessey was the lone occupant of the residence when the fire broke out.

A Florence couple, Mr. and Mrs. Frank Conrad, had passed the house enroute to Coolidge. Only a few minutes later as they were returning to Florence they discovered the blaze. According to Conrad, one side of the house was completely engulfed and the remainder caught on in just a few moments.

Cause of the fire has not been determined.

Efforts of neighbors and passers-by to establish a bucket brigade or to extinguish the flames by drawing water from an irrigation ditch proved to no avail.

Mr. Hennessey's son, George, was asleep in a small house trailer several feet away when the fire broke out.

Henry Edward Hennessey was born April 27, 1875 in Texas. He came to Arizona in 1911 and to the Florence-Coolidge district in 1941.

Mr. Hennessey was the first prison guard to retire under the retirement system at Arizona State Prison. He worked more than five years as a livestock sanitary inspector before becoming a guard in 1942. He retired in 1954.

During his work as a guard, he foiled the escape of an inmate on a work detail after a fellow guard had been taken hostage.

Surviving in addition to his son, George, is a daughter, Leola Finney of Show Low; a sister, Nellie Adams of Sunnyslope; a brother and sister, living out of state; 13 grandchildren; 25 great-grandchildren and four great-great-grandchildren.

Services were conducted by the Rev. Gary Weaver of the Community Presbyterian Church Wednesday in the Cole and Maud Chapel, Coolidge. Burial was at Valley Memorial Park.

## Water Report

At 7 a.m. today there were 411,551 acre feet available water storage behind Coolidge Dam. This represents an increase of 426 acre feet over Monday's total.

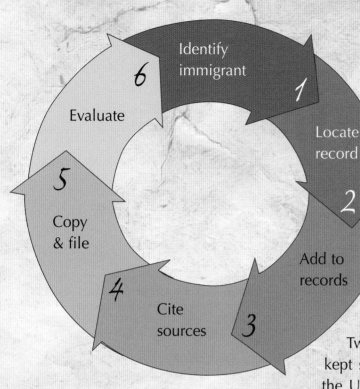

Identify immigrant

1

Locate record

2

Add to records

3

Cite sources

4

Copy & file

5

Evaluate

6

# How can I use immigration records & passenger lists?

## 30

### technique

Use the following six steps to obtain information from immigration records and passenger lists.

1. Identify the name and approximate age of your immigrant ancestor and the date when he arrived in the United States.

2. Locate the immigration record or passenger list he may be mentioned on.

3. Add information to your forms.

4. Cite the sources.

5. Copy and file the information with your records.

6. Evaluate data to see if the goal was met.

Two types of federal immigration records have been kept since 1820. Customs passenger lists were kept by the US Customs Service from 1820 until approximately 1891. Immigration passenger lists were kept by the US Immigration and Naturalization Service (INS) from 1906 until 1957.

When researching records for your immigrant ancestors, be aware that many immigrants changed or shortened their names when they arrived in America. Often they did this to make their names easier to spell or to sound less foreign. On occasion, the immigration clerk purposely shortened, or accidentally misspelled the name, and the emigrant kept the change.

After 1820, passenger arrival lists are the best source of immigration information. They provide the names and ages of the passenger, spouse, and family members; the name of the ship, the port from which it embarked, and the dates of departure and arrival.

Most of the 20th century ship records and passenger lists to the United States have been indexed and can be viewed in the microfilm collections at the National Archives. (Refer to What can I find in the Library of Congress? on page 51.) These records can also be viewed at the Family History Library. (Refer to What can I find in the Family History Library? on pages 48–49.)

| Names of passengers | Age | Sex | Occupation | Country to which they belong | Country of which they intend becoming inhabitants | Ship or vessel with the name of the master or commander |
|---|---|---|---|---|---|---|
| **CHARLESTON Cont.** | | | | | | |
| **Q. E. Sept. 30, 1823** | | | | | | |
| | | | | | | |
| A. Wishuby | 18 | M | Merchant | U. States | U. States | |
| Ab. Buckin * | 58 | M | Labourer | " | " | |
| Hodge Pinkney | 50 | M | Planter | " | " | |
| Wm. Peat | 30 | M | Mariner | " | " | Brig Ann. |
| Elias Wilkins | 40 | M | Farmer | " | " | Sch. Experiment. |
| Joshua Walker | 35 | M | " | " | " | |
| Robt. Beck & ch. | 35 | M | Joiner | " | " | |
| John Turnbull | 50 | M | Farmer | " | " | |
| Benedict Mispert | 60 | M | Cutler | Switzerland | " | Ship Eolus. Geer. |
| Jacob      " | 23 | M | " | " | " | |
| Samuel    " | 25 | M | Carpenter | " | " | |
| Lewis      " | 22 | M | Cutler | " | " | |
| Mary       " | 26 | F | | " | " | |
| Jacob Shelburn | 27 | M | Carpenter | " | " | |
| Jacob Hasches | 21 | M | Shoemaker | " | " | |
| John Buanard/Busnard | 24 | M | " | " | " | |
| --- Karns | 38 | M | Clockmaker | " | " | |
| --- Sigman | 39 | M | Shoemaker | " | " | |
| Charles Napier | 30 | M | " | " | " | |
| Fred. Shults | 20 | M | Farmer | " | " | |
| Joseph Spirer | 23 | M | Nailer | Germany | " | |
| B. Leshin | 45 | M | Hosier | " | " | |
| F. Narden | 42 | M | Miller | " | " | |
| L.   "   & 9 ch. | 41 | F | | " | " | |
| David " | 41 | M | " | " | " | |
| John Claude | 23 | M | Shoemaker | " | " | |
| C. Jaques | 56 | M | Farmer | " | " | |
| Mrs.   "   & 7 ch. | 42 | F | | " | " | |
| John Schimanke | 44 | M | " | " | " | |
| Mrs.    "   & 6 ch. | 36 | F | | " | " | |
| M. Nicherde | 43 | M | Carpenter | " | " | |
| Mrs.   "   & 4 ch. | 43 | F | | " | " | |
| | | | | | | |
| **NEW HAVEN** | | | | | | |
| **Q. E. Sept. 30, 1823** | | | | | | |
| | | | | | | |
| J. A. Anderson | 28 | M | Merchant | England | U. States | Brig Underhill. Clarke. |
| Geo. Mardenburgh | 50 | M | Planter | " | " | Brig Charles. Glenny. |
| Mary    "   & 2 ch. | 45 | F | | " | " | |
| John Guijer * | 30 | M | Merchant | " | " | |
| M. Divine | 29 | M | Farmer | " | " | Sch. Union. Gibbs. |
| Geo. Dougherty | 20 | M | " | " | " | |
| Wm. Gallagher | 25 | M | " | " | " | |
| Mary Flinn & ch. | 28 | F | | " | " | |

*1823 passenger list*

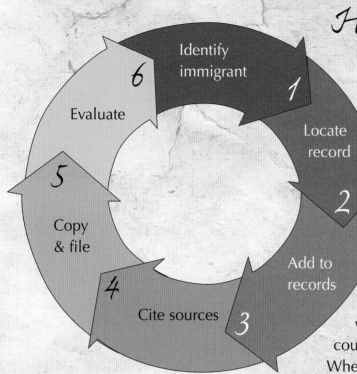

Identify immigrant 1

Locate record 2

Add to records 3

Cite sources 4

Copy & file 5

Evaluate 6

# How can I use naturalization & citizenship records?

Naturalization is the process of granting citizenship privileges and responsibilities to people who were born in other countries. Because settlers were welcomed in the American colonies, naturalization only consisted of oaths of allegiance for people coming from non-British lands. When a man was naturalized before 1920, his wife and minor children also became citizens. Naturalization records are held in the court of record where they were processed—that could be a federal, state, county, or municipal court.

When the United States was formed, Congress began to pass laws regulating naturalization. Since 1795, emigrants have been subject to a five-year process for becoming citizens. Later immigrants filed a declaration of intent. Five or more years after emigrating, immigrants petitioned for naturalization.

Of those whom applied, many did not complete the requirements for citizenship. Evidence that an immigrant completed citizenship requirements can be found in censuses, court minutes, homestead records, passports, voting registers, and military papers. Even if an immigrant ancestor did not complete the process and become a citizen, he may have filed an application. These application records still exist and can be helpful.

Older naturalization and citizenship records tell the country from which your ancestor emigrated, his foreign and Americanized names, residence, and date of arrival.

In 1906, these records were more detailed and included the birth dates and birth places, and the immigration information about the members of his family.

After 1920 these records included birth dates and origins for the emigrant and other family members, port of arrival, vessel name, and date of arrival.

# 31
## technique

Use the following six steps to obtain information from naturalization and citizenship records.

1. Identify the name and approximate age of your immigrant ancestors and the date when they arrived in the United States.

2. Locate the naturalization or citizenship record.

3. Add information to your forms.

4. Cite your sources.

5. Copy and file the information.

6. Evaluate data to see if the goal was met.

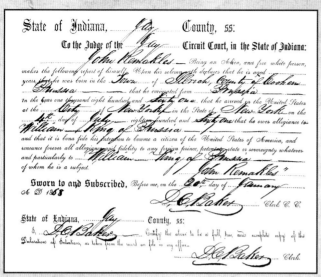

*1868 Immigration document*

*Courtesy of Carole Flygare Davidson*

*1939 Declaration of Intention*

*Section 4:*
*Unique uses of genealogy findings*

*Cynthia Doxy*

Cynthia Doxy, Ph.D., is an assistant professor of Church History and Doctrine at Brigham Young University in Provo, Utah. Research and interest in family history began when, as a child, she accompanied her mother to the genealogy library to search for ancestors. Although her educational background is in Family Studies, she has pursued family history as both a hobby and an occupation while teaching the Introduction to Family History course at BYU.

Cynthia uses genograms in her college lectures to illustrate to her students how traits and characteristics carry from one generation to the next. She admits this is not a new concept and, in fact, has used a number of sources to assist her in developing genograms for her teaching purposes.

# Genograms

The Sample Genogram shown on page 93 is a pictorial graph of the structure and characteristics of a family across three or more generations. A genogram may not replace the traditional pedigree charts and family group sheets for use in genealogical research; but it can provide a way to look beneath the surface of names, dates, and places so that genealogists can recognize family characteristics and patterns at a glance. Genograms track and illustrate traits carried from one generation to the next and are illustrated with easy-to-see-at-a-glance symbols. These symbols can be genetic such as inherited diseases, physical characteristics, religion, beliefs, or communication patterns.

Genograms have been used in health-care settings, social work, therapy studies, and for instilling a sense of identity and kinship.

By seeing family patterns in a genogram, individuals may realize their personal identity more fully by seeing themselves as part of a greater family network. As we learn more about family members, we begin to appreciate the role our ancestors played in our lives; and that we have a responsibility to do the same for our posterity, thus forging a link between past and future generations.

A genogram should track at least three generations. Gather information such as names of all persons, including the birth order and gender, marital status of couples, and any other pertinent information such as birth dates, marriage, divorce, and death. Using Possible Items to Track on page 94 as a guide, decide what information or traits you would like to track within your own family.

As you select these traits, assign a symbol to each trait or characteristic. These symbols are defined in the "legend" as the key for the genogram.

# Sample Genogram

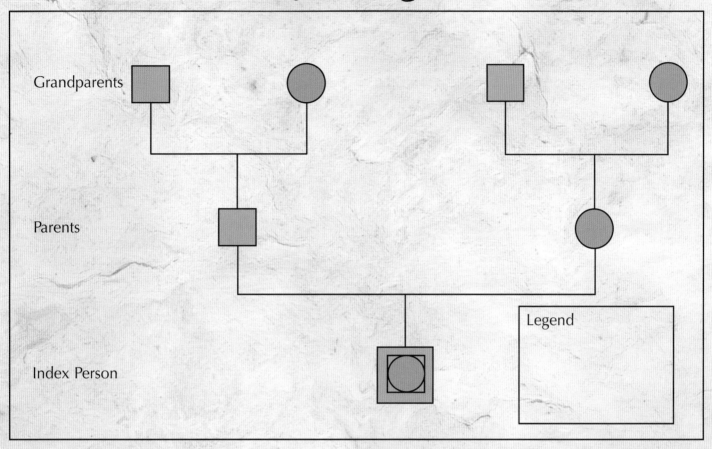

Grandparents

Parents

Index Person

Legend

Standardized symbols are:

• Squares represent males and circles represent females.

• Double lines around the square or circle indicate the index person.

• Names and dates are written above or below the symbol.

• An X inside a figure designates the person is deceased.

• Connecting lines going down and across denote married partners. The husband is on the left and the wife on the right.

• Divorce is indicated with two slashes (//) in the horizontal marriage line. The dates for marriage and divorce are written above the marriage line.

• Vertical lines are drawn below marriage lines for the children, with the oldest child on the left and the youngest on the right.

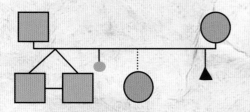

There are a variety of symbols used for special circumstances. Some of the most common are:

• Diverging lines connect twins to parents.

• Identical twins are connected by a bar between the children.

• Miscarriages are noted with a small filled-in circle.

• Dotted lines connect adopted children.

• Pregnancies are illustrated by a triangle.

## Possible Items to Track

**Socioeconomic Characteristics**
Occupation
Education level
Community service

**Religious Values**
Church affiliation
Church leadership
Church volunteer service

**Cultural Background**
Country of origin
Languages spoken
Cultural arts, practices, and traditions
Naming patterns

**Genetic/Environmental Factors**
Artistic, musical, literary abilities
Personality traits: frugality, love, consideration for others, friendliness, etc.

**Family Values**
Family closeness
Desire for learning or education
Preferences for politics. material goods, food, work ethic, athletic teams, etc.

Select genogram web sites:
www.genealogytoday.com/articles/genogram.html—describes genograms focusing on family health.

www.smartdraw.com/specials/genealogy.asp?id=24226—the SmartDraw Program draws genograms.

www.genogram.freeservers.com/index.html—the site explains Family Systems Theory, and those who created genograms.

www.multiculturalfamily.org/Genograms.htm—using genograms for multicultural families.

www.stepfamilyinfo.org/03/geno1.htm—using genograms for step-families.

# Johnson Family Genogram

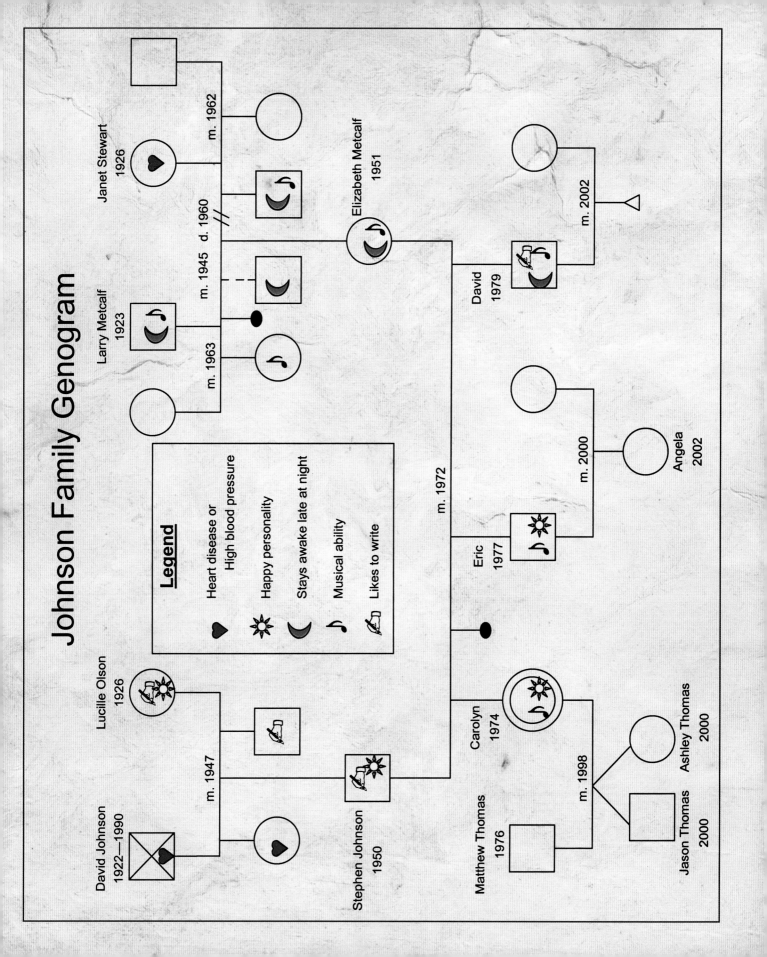

above: The facial features between generations tell a story in these photographs.

below: Four generations are pictured and displayed above the mantel, along with the candleholders that each of the first three generations used in their wedding ceremonies.

# Family photography

Photographs used as part of the decor of a home preserves the fond memories of loved family members. The stories and legends of parents, grandparents, and forefathers are also honored.

Rather than tucking photographs away in memory albums and scrapbooks, make family members and events an integral part of your daily lifestyle. Decorate each room with unique framing and photograph-display treatments styled to enhance the personality of each portrait and the space where it will be viewed. Let your home reflect a love that invites all who enter to feel a strong sense of family, warmth, and welcome.

Family members, especially children, remain constant yet change in the blink of an eye. Capture on a regular basis candid shots of the stages through which your family members travel.

Photographs should not be taken only in a photographer's studio, but in a natural surrounding that is part of you and your family. Since people are not structured sets with contrived backgrounds, they should be captured as the hikers, boaters, or car aficionados they are.

Candid shots bring your family members to life, by catching them in true situations. An unposed photograph of your family members interacting can capture their mannerisms, expressions, actions, and interactions with one another.

*left: When searching and preserving family histories, do not forget the living family members. Photograph and record the events, candid times, and special moments experienced by your family. By using this photography, you are able to "scrapbook" the walls of your home and tell the story of your family's life.*

*below: The mantel is commonly used to display photographs. Different colors, shapes, and sizes of frames will add to the diversity which is prevalent in the photographs themselves.*

When favorite pictures are kept in shoe boxes, lab envelopes, or scrapbooks, they are more difficult to share. If they are taken from these hiding places and enlarged, cropped, tinted, digitally enhanced, copied, and creatively framed, they become more than snapshots in an album. They become works of art that evoke emotions and give life to a family.

*above: Unique frames can be a way of sharing the complexities of the framed person. This half-frame was constructed, then weighted to become a bookend. The bookend blends with the room's decor while securely holding the books the subject holds dear.*

*left: Your current family is an important part of your family history now and in the years to come. This current family photograph was enlarged to 30" x 40" and is proudly displayed above this stone fireplace.*

*above: Whether it is a daily routine or a special event, the activities that fill your hours from morning until night become a part of you. Family photographs should be taken throughout the days. Whatever the occasion or activity, snapshots will remind you and later family members of your lifestyle, likes, passions, and associations.*

*below: To show the passage of time, these photographs of brother and sisters show the way they were then and the way they are now.*

*above: Every year a new frame is converted into a Christmas ornament. A different family member is honored and the ornament is added to the cherished ornaments that hang from the family tree.*

When displaying photographs of your progenitors do not lock them into one age. Do not only display the photograph of your grandmother in her 80s. Through a variety of pictures, enjoy her youthful smile in her teens or her awareness as a baby. Whatever photographs are available to you can add to the life and times of a past relative.

# Heritage scrapbooking

Creating scrapbooks are a means of preserving and protecting memories as well as personal or family histories. Scrapbooking as a hobby not only provides a creative outlet for the designer, but also promotes a sense of belonging for those whose lives and accomplishments are creatively chronicled and compiled into an album. Living family members are also an integral part of the family's history and should be documented just as those who have gone on before.

*top left:* A die-cut train, postage stamp from the period, and letter, all celebrate the life of the man honored in this collage.

*top right:* This photo album cover has been embellished with keepsakes of a memorable family road trip.

*below:* A wide variety of photographs are chronicled and intermingled to connect the generations. Ribbons, gold markings, and sponging techniques symbolize the depth the subjects deserve.

MEMORY IS YOUR LINK WITH THE CENTURIES. ALL THAT MEN HAVE REMEMBERED AND SET DOWN IN PRINT THROUGH THE AGES IS A PRECIOUS LEGACY TO YOU. THE MIRACLE OF MEMORY GIVES CONTINUITY TO LIFE.

Bits of fabric, ribbon, lace paper, international stamps, postcards, and torn papers are layered together to create a beautiful collage symbolizing the events of a couple's photographed life together.

top left: This collage is made up of layers of decoratively cut papers. Portions of a letter and its envelope are the central focal point with photographs of the recipient surrounding the letter.

top right: This three-generation photograph is surrounded by beaded lace layered over light fabric and enhanced with embroidered ribbon flowers.

bottom left: This photo border was created using gold-painted card stock covered with decorative tissue paper and randomly torn oriental lace paper.

bottom right: This photo was placed within an enlarged print of a postcard, which had been enhanced with sponging and gold acrylic paint.

# Historic homes

Craig Call is from Soda Springs, Idaho, and is the great-great-grandson of Ebenezer and Phoebe Richardson. Janine Winder Call hails from Craig, Colorado. They met in college before embarking on a long odyssey with old buildings and varied careers.

Craig has been President of the Utah Heritage Foundation and chaired the Idaho Heritage Trust. He also helped found the organization to restore the historic Chesterfield Townsite in Idaho. Craig has restored more than two dozen buildings that are listed on the National Register of Historic Places.

Janine is currently a schoolteacher and Craig is an attorney. They live in Plain City, Utah, in a restored "saltbox" style home built in 1862.

*Craig & Janine Call and family*

*Saltbox home, 1862*

*Saltbox home, 1994*

The "old rock house," pictured above, has been home to many for over 150 years and was built for William Dolby and Caroline Skeen in 1862. Skeen and his father, Joseph, were among the first settlers in Plain City in 1859. The Skeens were originally from Lancaster County, Pennsylvania, an area known for its Amish farms and historic countryside dotted with homes of stone built much like this one. The shape of this home is New England in derivation and known as the saltbox style, since the front of the home is larger than the back and the rear roof is longer and ends lower than it does in the front, assuring that heavy snows slide off the back of the house. Only a few of the early

Utah saltbox homes remain standing today.

The stones for this home came from the mountains at Hot Springs, Wyoming, in a wagon pulled by oxen—at least 200 wagon loads—enough to build a house 28 feet by 38 feet that stands one and a half stories tall. The walls are two feet thick.

By 1868, the Skeens sold the home to Ebenezer Richardson. Richardson was a polygamist and had two wives who were sisters, Polly Ann and Phoebe Wooster. These women moved in with a combined family of 12 children. Only one of the children was a girl so she slept in a bedroom on the main floor. The eleven boys slept in the big unfinished loft of the house, which looks today just like it did then—bare rock walls, uninsulated ceiling, and no heat except for the stovepipes that come through from the floor. Heating was always by stoves. It never had indoor plumbing or extensive wiring.

The Richardson family occupied the home until the 1950s. For more than 85 years, four generations of Richardsons enjoyed the shelter and strength of this robust home. About 1955, it was determined to be obsolete and left vacant.

For 40 years the house was preserved by Dean Baker. It served as a storage area and barn for a awhile. There was considerable vandalism over the

*Refurbished bathroom*

*Before refurbishing*

*Refurbished sitting room*

years; but in 1972 Nelda and Jack Etherington purchased the home and put a new roof on it, saving it from major deterioration. Both Baker and Etherington are descendants of William Dolby Skeen. In 1994 the Etheringtons sold the house to Craig and Janine Call.

The Calls restored the old house and added the new wing to the south, which provides additional living space. They were able to restore the original floor plan and preserve the historic woodwork. Wherever possible, the hardware and fixtures replicate the original 1862 appearance.

As they excavated the crawl space under the old floors, the Calls sifted the dirt and found hundreds of artifacts. Marbles, spools, china pieces, leather, buttons, and many other bits and pieces of history came out of the dust to show life in a previous century.

*Sifting through the floor dirt*

*Found objects dug up from the dirt floor*

*The Skeen-Richardson House, above, has been restored and is currently listed on the National Register of Historic Places. The house is connected to a newly built home with all the latest amenities.*

# Glossary

**Administrator**—court-appointed person who handles the business of a deceased person's estate.

**Ancestor**—people from whom one is descended, especially a relative more distant than a grandparent.

**Archives**—a depository containing retired official records of public or private agencies.

**Associated families**—individuals who traveled, attended church, and intermarried with and witnessed legal documents for the families being researched.

**Baptism or christening**—commonly the ordinance associated with the naming of a baby.

**Biography**—important events of a person's life written as a narrative.

**Census**—the counting or listing of inhabitants of a certain region; done on a federal or state basis.

**Collateral relatives**—people who share an ancestor but do not descend from one another.

**Compiled source**—information abstracted from various original documents into one record.

**Correspondence log**—form to keep track of requests for genealogical data from relatives and repositories.

**Death notice**—a short mention of a person's death, briefer than an obituary.

**Deed**—a legal document transferring real property.

**Depository**—a library designated to receive U.S. government documents.

**Descendant**—one who descends from an ancestor.

**Direct ancestor or direct line**—persons whose names appear on one's pedigree chart.

**Emigration**—the act of moving from one country or area to another.

**End-of-line**—When, after extensive research, you cannot identify the parents of an ancestor.

**Enumeration order**—the sequence in which census entries were recorded; normally house to house.

**Enumerators**—the individuals who recorded censuses.

**Estate**—property held by a person at the time of his death.

**Executor**—the person named in a will to handle the affairs of an estate after the death of the deviser.

**Extract**—to copy a record, or portions of a record, verbatim from a record.

**Family group sheet**—a standard chart for recording genealogical information about one family.

**Family History Center**—one of many genealogy resource libraries operated by the LDS Church, where a visitor can access the records located at the Family History Library in Salt Lake City, Utah.

**Family History Library**—depository of the largest collection of genealogical records in the world.

**Family tradition**—stories and legends verbally handed down through generations.

**Genealogy**—the study of family descent.

**Generation**—all the offspring that are at the same stage of descent from a common ancestor.

**Genogram**—pictorial graph showing structure and characteristics of a specific sample group.

**Head of household**—the person whose name appears first in the census enumeration of a family.

**Heirloom**—a sentimental object passed down, from generation to generation.

**Immigrant ancestor**—the first person in an ancestral line to settle in America.

**Immigration**—the act of coming into one country or area from another, usually to settle.

**In-law**—person related by marriage or by another legal tie.

**Intestate**—describing a case where a person dies leaving no valid will.

**Inventory**—a list of the property held by a person at the time of his death.

**Issue**—children of a couple.

**Local history**—the events of the past that impact a certain area; often includes family histories.

**Microfiche**—a sheet of microfilm preserving a considerable number of printed pages in reduced form.

**Microfilm**—a film on which printed materials are photographed.

**National Archives**—the depository for documents relating to the history and people of the United States.

**Naturalization records**—documents produced when an immigrant becomes a citizen of the United States.

**Neighbors**—those who appear to reside in the same vicinity as the family being researched.

**Obituary**—an announcement of a person's death, giving details about the deceased's origins, biographical data, survivors, religion, and burial information.

**Original source**—an historical document in its original form.

**Pedigree**—one's ancestry or lineage.

**Pedigree chart**—chart used to record genealogical information.

**Pension**—a stipend provided to an elderly or disabled military veteran, or to his widow or children.

**Periodical**—publication issued at regular intervals.

**Personal property**—possessions held by a person, which may include livestock, gold watches, carriages, and slaves.

**Plat**—a map of the cemetery showing the locations of each grave and who owns it.

**Political boundary**—the borders of a governmental jurisdiction.

**Primary source**—a record created at the time of an event, usually by someone with personal knowledge.

**Probate**—the legal process of transferring items of a deceased person's estate to heirs.

**Progenitor**—the earliest known ancestor in one's lineage.

**Real property**—land.

**Reapportionment**—periodic redrawing of geographic boundaries.

**Record depository**—a place where records are kept for safekeeping, including libraries, archives, or government and church offices.

**Research log**—a written document listing records searched and information found.

*Wouldn't it be interesting to see the photograph Ichabod Adams is holding in this picture?*

**Secondary source**—record containing information compiled long after the events discussed; generally not as reliable as a primary source.

**Sexton**—the person whose job it is to maintain the cemetery and prepare for burials.

**Source citation**—a note stating where specific information was derived.

**Surname**—family name or last name.

**Tax record**—list of people paying taxes in a given area, with a list of their property; usually compiled annually on a county level.

**Testate**—describing a case where a person dies leaving a valid will.

**Transcript**—a verbatim copy of a record.

**Vital records**—records of births, deaths, marriages, and divorces.

**Will**—legal document providing for the disposition of a person's property.

# Bibliography

*A Guide to Research*
The Church of Jesus Christ of Latter-day Saints, 1994

*Ancestors–Guide to Discovery*
Jim Tyrrell, KBYU TV, 2000

*Building an American Pedigree*
Norman E. Wright,
Brigham Young University Press, 1974

*Genealogy Is More Than Charts*
Lorna Duane Smith, LifeTimes, 1991

*The Unpuzzling Your Past Workbook*
Emily Anne Croom, Betterway Books, 1996

Is this really what you call a family tree with leaves and limbs, trunks, and roots to see? Or is it not the ones we cherish though parts may weaken and even perish.

Is it not the love we feel that sustains us through the troubled years and helps us find the gold in all our tears.

*Courtesy of Bert Ostlund*

# Internet resources

There are myriad web sites relating to genealogy. Some of the most popular are:

**www.Ancestry.com** links to a number of sites, including the Social Security Death Index.

**www.archives.ca/** links to the National Archives of Canada.

**www.Cyndislist.com** links to more than 59,000 sites.

**www.FamilySearch.org** links to ancestral file, international genealogical index, and the card catalog for the Family History Library in Salt Lake City, Utah.

**www.gendex.com/gendex/** searches more than 1800 on-line genealogical databases.

**www.genealogy.com** links to other historical sites.

**www.genealogysitefinder.com** identifies over 76,000 on-line genealogical sites.

**www.lcweb.loc.gov** links to the Library of Congress.

**www.nara.gov** links to the National Archives and Records Administration site.

**www.pro.gov.uk/** links to Public Record Office for the United Kingdom.

**www.rootsweb.com** is the oldest genealogy site and surname list.

**www.stylscript.com** links to calligraphy works of Susan Nelson

**www.usgenweb.com** links to counties and states.

**www.USGenWeb.org** provides leads for historical and genealogical data on counties.

**www.worldgenweb.org** links to other countries.

# About the author

Laura has always had a passion for researching and studying her family history. Growing up with family stories told at her grandmothers' knees and enjoying traditions and stories, she has always felt a kinship to her ancestors.

Laura lives in Utah with her four daughters and spends her time writing and designing books on many topics. She has published numerous magazine articles on travel, food, and children's fiction. She enjoys preserving the stories of her ancestors and enjoys visiting the various gravesites and family homesteads of those who came before her.

# Special thanks to

My beautiful daughters Christie, Lisa, Katie, and Sara for making life a joy.
My mother, Jill, for her constant support.
My publisher and friend, Jo Packham, for seeing the vision of this book.
Lon Elbert for his insight and research time.
Blaine Robinson for keeping my passion for this project alive.
Bill Woodruff at The Church of Jesus Christ of Latter-day Saints for his review.
Those willing to share their treasures:
Carolyn Apsley, Areta Bingham, Craig & Janine Call, Carole Davidson, Cynthia Doxey, Connie Duran, Susan Fredrick, Cynthia Gaufin, Mary Gillette, JoAnn Hatch, Ryne Hazen, Jill Hennessey, Paul & Julina Hokanson, Chris Little, Susan Nelson, Bert & Margaret Ostlund, Sharon Reynolds, Kim Taylor

# Dedication

To my "Honey" grandma (left) who taught me to work with my hands and the worth of family, and to my grandma Fanny (right) who was my example of grace, service, and perseverance.

# Index